The generous support of
JOAN AND PETER ANDREWS
for this exhibition publication is
gratefully acknowledged.

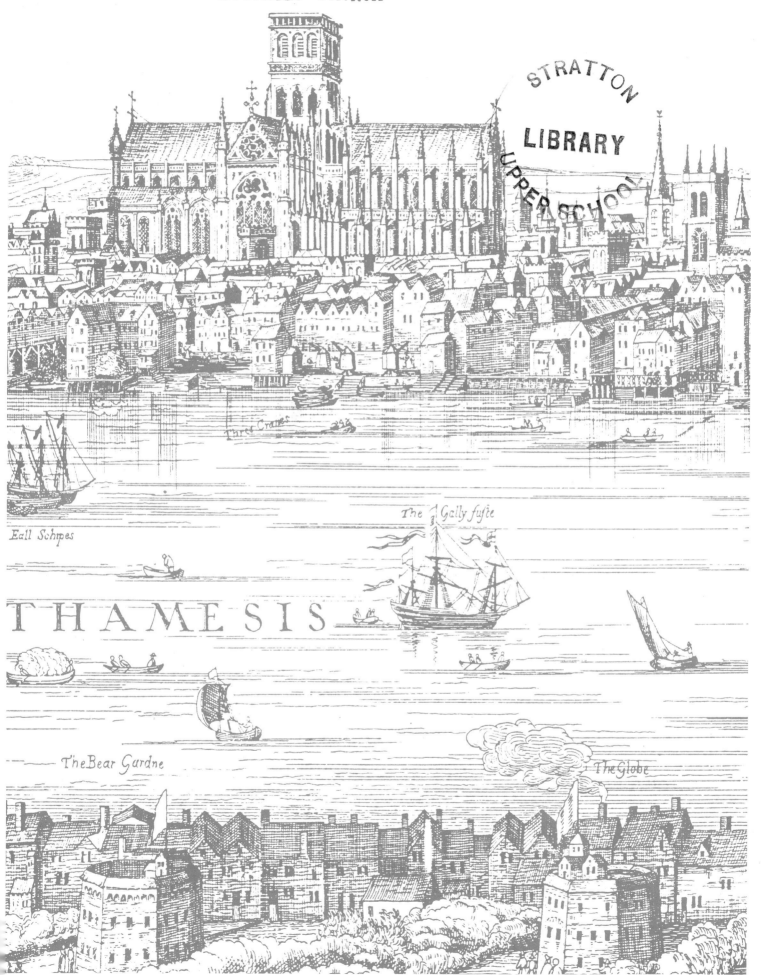

S. PAULES CHURCH

THAMESIS

Three Cranes

The Gally fuſte

Eall Schipes

The Bear Gardne

The Globe

In conjunction with
the exhibition
THE FIRST FOLIO OF SHAKESPEARE
at the
Folger Shakespeare Library
Washington, D.C.
April 1, 1991—September 21, 1991

The First Folio
of Shakespeare

Ex Dono Will. Iaggard Typographi a° 1623

MR. WILLIAM
SHAKESPEARES

COMEDIES,
HISTORIES, &
TRAGEDIES.

Published according to the True Originall Copies.

LONDON
Printed by Isaac Iaggard, and Ed. Blount. 1623.

Peter W. M. Blayney

The Folger Shakespeare Library is
administered by the Trustees of
Amherst College.

Werner Gundersheimer, Director

Rachel Doggett, Andrew W. Mellon Curator of Books

Folger Library Publications is a
program of the Division of Museum
and Public Programs.

Janet Alexander Griffin, Director

Jane Bissonnette, Assistant

Julie Ainsworth, Photographer

Library of Congress Catalog Card Number: 91-71161
ISBN 0-9629254-3-8

Printed in the United States of America
by Hagerstown Bookbinding and Printing Company
Hagerstown, Maryland.
Cover designed by Jeanne Krohn, Krohn Design, Inc.

Foreword

The Folger Shakespeare Library is known for many things, but its most celebrated distinction is the possession of approximately one-third of the surviving First Folios of Shakespeare's plays. Many people know this, but relatively few can provide a coherent definition of a First Folio, let alone an explanation of the significance of these notable volumes.

The ignorance that surrounds the First Folio is not limited to the general public. Indeed, the book enjoys almost totemic status among book collectors and the legions of the Bard's devotees; and like a ritual object, it has been allowed to exist within an aura of mystery, if not actual mystification. Surely there is something remarkable about the fact that of the many thousands of early English imprints in the Folger Library, the Folios are the only books that have never been catalogued. Only in the last few months has the Library undertaken the first steps needed to remedy this situation.

Moreover, we at the Folger have done our share to contribute to the sense of awe surrounding the Folios. By long-established custom, we exhibit *one* of them in the Great Hall, so that the public may see *an* example of this treasure of civilization. This emphasis on the uniqueness of the First Folio is a bit misleading, and for us, perhaps even a bit self-serving. The plain truth is that the First Folio, leaving aside its indisputable cultural importance, is not a particularly rare book. This library possesses thousands of books which are far less common (most of them not nearly as important, to be sure).

Yet the First Folio is a landmark publication in terms of the preservation and editing of Shakespeare's plays, as well as the history of the book. This exhibition explains precisely why and how this is so. Its curator, Peter W. M. Blayney, has selected 24 of the Folger's First Folios, together with four fragments, in order to illuminate their similarities and differences. In analyzing the Folios—both in their cases and in the text of this masterly essay—Dr. Blayney puts his vast knowledge of the subject at our disposal, often with the energy and deductive skill of a detective. He notices how Folios differed from one another even as they left the printing house in 1623, how they then proceeded to develop individual traits as they passed in and out of the hands of binders, booksellers, and different (and indifferent!) owners across the centuries. He explains how a book like this was made, by whom, and for whom; what it cost, and what effects changing attitudes toward Shakespeare had on the edition's preservation. He interprets the activities of Mr. and Mrs. Folger as collectors, and reveals how their particular values and insights both derived from and helped to shape the views of their contemporaries.

In short, Dr. Blayney, who probably knows more about the London book trade in the Age of Shakespeare than anyone else now living, makes the Folios and their economic, social, and intellectual history accessible to us in a highly original and compelling way. In the course of his research for this exhibition, he has made a number of intriguing discoveries about individual Folios. But this booklet is not addressed to specialists. Unlike much of the scholarly work accompanying exhibitions these days, it can be read for fun and profit by anyone with an interest in the subject.

Dr. Blayney deserves our thanks, not only for wearing his learning so lightly, but also for almost single-handedly preparing the materials for this exhibition. As a true disciple of the printers of Jacobean London, he designed and prepared camera-ready copy for the labels and for this brochure. A sincere word of appreciation also goes to Julie Ainsworth, Head of Photography, who produced over 60 photographs for this exhibition, many of them requiring painstaking effort. J. Franklin Mowery and his able brigade of conservators have once again balanced the sometimes competing claims of safety, accessibility, and style.

This exhibition provides a unique opportunity—available nowhere else on earth—to learn about and to enjoy a very remarkable publication. I hope that you will share my enthusiasm for it.

Werner Gundersheimer
Director

The First Folio of Shakespeare

In November 1623, seven years after William Shakespeare had died at his home in Stratford-upon-Avon, a book containing 36 of his plays was published in London. The book was a large folio (a format with pages about as wide as those of a modern encyclopædia, but two or three inches taller), and nothing quite like it had ever been published in folio before.

The folio format was usually reserved for works of reference (on such subjects as theology, law, history, and heraldry) and for the collected writings of important authors, both ancient (Homer, Tacitus, Saint Augustine) and modern (Spenser, Sir Philip Sidney, Bishop Joseph Hall). Plays written for the public theatres, however, were generally viewed as fairly trivial works of popular entertainment, unworthy of serious consideration as literature. In 1616 Ben Jonson had included nine plays in a folio collection of his 'Workes', and several of his contemporaries had jokingly suggested that he had forgotten the difference between 'work' and 'play'. The First Folio of 1623 was not only the first collected edition of Shakespeare—it was the first folio book ever published in England that was devoted exclusively to plays.

Of the 36 plays in the Folio, 14 had already been printed as separate play-quartos containing texts of reasonably high quality. Only two of those plays were simply reprinted in the Folio: six were reprinted from copies that had been at least partly edited by comparison with manuscripts owned by the players (who collaborated in the publication), and six were newly printed from manuscripts that differed more or less widely from the earlier printed editions. Four of the remaining 22 plays had been printed only as what are now called 'Bad Quartos', in which the texts had been substantially abridged (possibly for performance) and at least partly corrupted (possibly by being reconstructed from memory). In the Folio, each of those four plays was printed from a full-length manuscript whose contents more closely resembled what Shakespeare had originally written.

None of the remaining 18 plays in the Folio had ever been printed before. Two anonymous plays published during the 1590s are sometimes claimed to be adaptations, corrupt texts, or first drafts of Shakespeare's *King John* and *The Taming of the Shrew*, but both are more probably old plays used by Shakespeare only as source material. Another play was apparently abridged, adapted, translated, and eventually published in 1620 by a touring company of English actors who were popular in Germany during Shakespeare's lifetime. But although the German text of *Julio und Hyppolita* was printed three years before the Folio, it would hardly be realistic to describe it as 'the first edition' of *The Two Gentlemen of Verona*.

Regrettably, the Folio did not include all of Shakespeare's known plays. *Pericles*, published under his name in 1609, has long been accepted as a Bad Quarto of a play written at least partly by Shakespeare, and *The Two Noble Kinsmen* (published in 1634 as the work of Shakespeare and John Fletcher) has more recently been accepted into the canon. So, too, has part of a manuscript play called *Sir Thomas More*, in which three pages of the unfinished revisions are widely believed to be in Shakespeare's handwriting. A play entitled *Love's Labours Won* was attributed to Shakespeare in 1598 and listed in a bookseller's daybook in 1603, but it has either been lost or has survived only under another title. Three manuscripts of a play called *Cardenio*, probably by Shakespeare and Fletcher, reputedly survived into the eighteenth century, but that play is now known only from an adaptation published in 1728.

Of the 39 plays now accepted as either wholly or partly by Shakespeare, 18 have survived *only* because the First Folio was published. Four more would otherwise have survived only in abridged and inferior versions, and at least half the remainder would have survived in versions differing more or less markedly from the texts we know today. It is hardly surprising that the First Folio has been called 'incomparably the most important work in the English language'.

PUBLISHERS, PLAYERS, AND PLANNING

We do not know whether the idea of publishing the Folio was first conceived by the players or the publishers, but the two groups had to cooperate before the idea became a reality. The publishers had most to gain if the venture succeeded; the players had almost nothing to lose if it failed. For most of his career, Shakespeare had been a shareholding member of the company that became the King's Men in 1603 (formerly the Lord Chamberlain's Men). His surviving fellows would have welcomed the planned edition as a tribute and memorial to one of the company's most successful playwrights. Furthermore, while relatively few of his plays may have remained in regular performance by the 1620s, the book would remind the public that many once-popular plays were still available to be revived on demand.

There was also money to be made—although not enough to suggest that the players' main motive was financial. Publishers sometimes negotiated contracts resembling royalty agreements among themselves, but when they bought 'copy' from non-members of the Stationers' Company, they usually purchased it outright. For the use of their manuscripts by the printer of the Folio, the players would have received only a single payment that is unlikely to have exceeded £50 and may well have been less.

The principal publishers, Edward Blount and Isaac Jaggard, would have hoped to make a considerably larger profit, but the venture was a risky one. As well as paying for the use of the playhouse manuscripts, they needed either to buy or to lease the publishing rights to the plays already in print. Those rights differed materially from modern 'copyright', and protected more than just the precise content of a particular work. If the owner of either *The Taming of a Shrew* or *The Troublesome Reign of King John* still had a large stock of unsold copies, he could legitimately complain that the

Shakespearean version might make them unsaleable, thus infringing his rights. Blount and Jaggard therefore also needed to negotiate with the owners of those plays.

No matter how many copies were printed, the cost per copy of the paper and printing would be essentially the same, but each copy sold would have to recover its proportional share of the fixed cost of acquiring the plays. If too few copies were printed, the book might fail to sell because it was overpriced; if too many were printed, the publishers might not sell enough copies to recover their costs. The ideal size of the edition could only be guessed, because there was no real precedent. Jonson's *Workes* of 1616, which apparently cost 9 or 10 shillings unbound (or 13–14 shillings in a plain calf binding) could not be used as a reliable guide to the probable demand. It had by no means sold out during the six years before work began on the Shakespeare collection, and it would not be reprinted until 1640. The Shakespeare Folio cost more to produce (it contained 60 fewer leaves, but was printed on larger paper, in two columns of smaller type), and sold for more than half as much again as the Jonson volume. The usual estimate of 1200 copies is unrealistically high. The fact that the book was reprinted after only nine years suggests a relatively small edition—probably no more than 750 copies, and perhaps fewer.

THE BLIND PRINTER AND HIS SON

Blount and Jaggard had no difficulty in choosing a printer. Isaac's father, William Jaggard, had set up a small printing house in 1604 near that of James Roberts. When Roberts retired in 1606, William bought and moved into the larger establishment, which was outside the city wall, on the corner of Aldersgate Street and the Barbican. By 1616 Isaac had begun to take an active part in managing the business, and by 1620 he had probably taken over

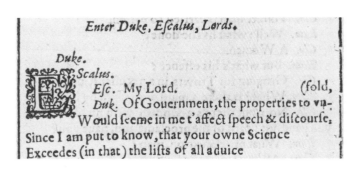

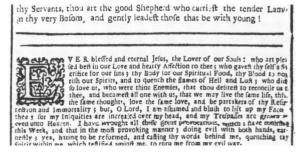

As the map opposite shows, Jaggard's printing house survived the Great Fire of London, and some of the ornamental blocks used in the Folio were still being used by Benjamin Motte in the eighteenth century. The initial 'E' used in Measure for Measure, *for example, is also found in a Motte type-specimen of 1713. (Cambridge University Library: reproduced by permission of the Syndics.)*

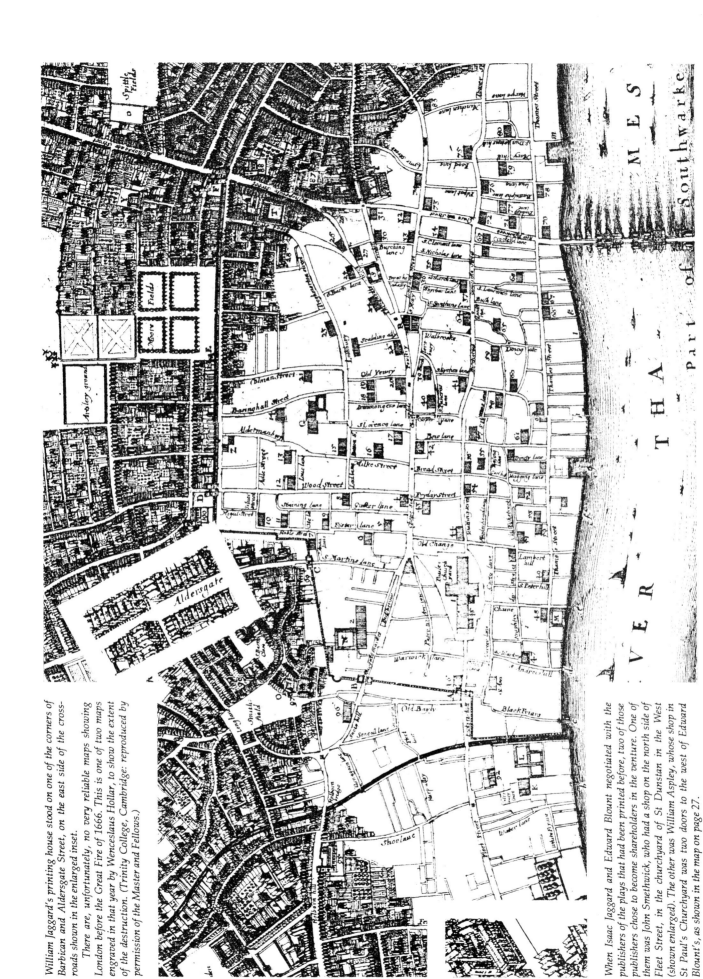

William Jaggard's printing house stood on one of the corners of Barbican and Aldersgate Street, on the east side of the cross-roads shown in the enlarged inset.

There are, unfortunately, no very reliable maps showing London before the Great Fire of 1666. This is one of two maps engraved in that year by Wenceslaus Hollar, to show the extent of the destruction. (Trinity College, Cambridge: reproduced by permission of the Master and Fellows.)

When Isaac Jaggard and Edward Blount negotiated with the publishers of the plays that had been printed before, two of those publishers chose to become shareholders in the venture. One of them was John Smethwick, who had a shop on the north side of Fleet Street, in the churchyard of St Dunstan in the West (shown enlarged). The other was William Aspley, whose shop in St Paul's Churchyard was two doors to the west of Edward Blount's, as shown in the map on page 27.

3

much of the responsibility for the day-to-day operations. William was still very much in control of his printing house until he died (shortly before the Folio was finished), but by 1623 he had been blind for several years.

William Jaggard had been involved in an earlier attempt to print a collected edition of Shakespeare. His friend Thomas Pavier had acquired the rights to several Shakespearean and other plays, and in 1619 he hired Jaggard to print what was intended to be a one-volume collection of reprinted quartos, beginning with the 'Bad' texts of *Henry VI* (parts 2 and 3) and *Pericles*. When the players learned what was afoot, they attempted to prevent it, perhaps because they were already thinking of compiling their own Shakespeare collection. In May 1619 the Lord Chamberlain instructed the Stationers' Company that no plays belonging to the King's Men should be printed without their consent. Pavier reacted by persuading Jaggard to reprint seven more of the quartos with false dates, so that they could be passed off as remainders of earlier editions.

Some scholars have found it strange that Jaggard should nevertheless have been considered an acceptable printer for the Folio. The players, however, had continued to deal with him since 1619,

because he held the monopoly for printing their playbills—and even if they knew that the reprints were falsely dated, they may not have known who printed them. Jaggard was, moreover, the best possible person to negotiate acceptable terms with Pavier (who owned four of the plays to be included in the Folio) and with two other publishers (each owning one play) who had probably also been involved in the illicit activities of 1619.

HOW THE PRINTING WAS RECONSTRUCTED

Much of what is now known about the printing of the First Folio is owed to the monumental study undertaken by Charlton K. Hinman. Using a special viewer that he designed and built himself, Hinman made a minutely detailed page-by-page comparison of 55 of the Folger copies. He also spent several years investigating and analyzing the patterns in which various recognizable objects reappeared throughout the book: each individual brass rule used in the box-frames around the text (identifiable by tell-tale bends and breaks); each separate setting of the running-titles used in each play; and hundreds of distinctively damaged types in the text itself. As a result, he was able to

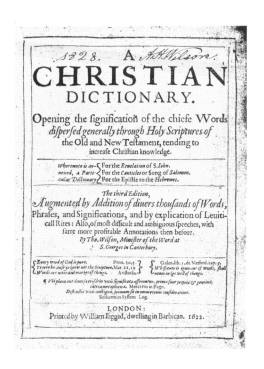

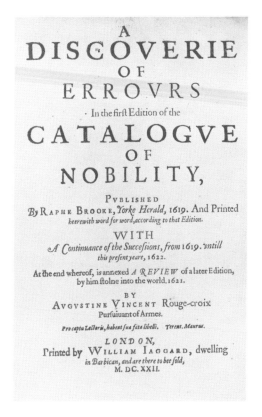

reconstruct the order in which the pages were set and printed, to identify which of several workmen set each page, and to relate many of the irregularities in the work to specific parts of other books that were being printed at the same time.

Hinman's study, *The Printing and Proof-Reading of the First Folio of Shakespeare*, was published in 1963. Since then, others have modified, corrected, and supplemented some of his conclusions, but his work remains an irreplaceable landmark in Shakespeare studies. While the following account differs in a few respects, most of it is derived from Hinman's reconstruction.

JAGGARD'S OTHER BOOKS OF 1622–3

The printing of the Shakespeare Folio began in early 1622, perhaps at the beginning of February, when Jaggard was still working on two books that had been started in 1621. One of them—an edition of Thomas Wilson's *Christian Dictionary*—was almost complete, and would be finished at about the same time as the third of the Folio Comedies. The other was still a long way from completion, and would not be finished until late November or early December. That book—Augustine Vincent's

Discoverie of Errors—was of greater importance to William Jaggard than was the First Folio.

In 1619 Jaggard had printed a book of noble pedigrees by Ralph Brooke, York Herald. By the time it was finished, Brooke had belatedly noticed some factual errors, which he corrected in a list of errata that implicitly blamed Jaggard for all the mistakes. Even so, his fellow heralds soon noticed that although the unpopular Brooke had always enjoyed heaping scorn on the mistakes of others, his own book was positively riddled with errors. Jaggard's personal friend Augustine Vincent, Rouge-Croix Pursuivant of Arms, began to compile a damning list, and Jaggard agreed to reprint Brooke's work with Vincent's critical commentary incorporated. When Brooke found what was being planned, he persuaded another printer to rush out a hasty reprint of his own, with a few new corrections and a new attempt to blame Jaggard for most of the mistakes. When Vincent's *Discoverie* finally appeared, the preliminaries included a lengthy open letter to Brooke, written in understandable anger by Jaggard himself.

At about the same time as he began printing the Folio, Jaggard started work on another large book—a translation from the French of André Favyn's *Theater of Honour*. Until December 1622

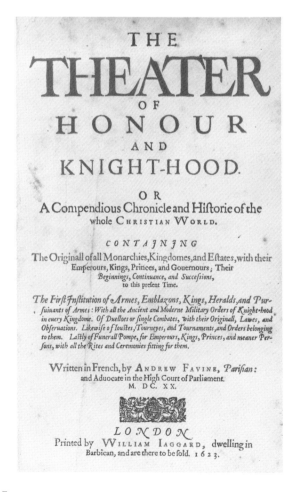

Moreouer, in citing Scriptures, I haue sometimes noted such places wherein the word which I doe interprete is onely named; Sometime, the place where the interpretation is found with the word, and some places which onely haue the interpretation, and not the word. I cite few places, because a light giuen to a word in one place, will cleare other places, where that word is vsed in the same sence, which the aduised Reader shall discerne by the cir-

narie : yet there has beene Knights, and Lords, and Gentlemen, with their Coaches; I warrant you Coach after Coach, letter after letter, gift after gift, smelling so sweetly, all Muske, and so rushing, I warrant you, in silke and golde, and in such alligant termes, and in such wine and suger of the best, and the fairest, that would haue wonne any womans heart: and I warrant you, they could neuer get an eye-winke of her: I had my selfe twentie

After a group of pages had been printed, the type was scrubbed clean. Each page was then dismantled line by line, and distributed letter by letter back into the right compartments of the type-case.

As was usual, the last pages of Wilson's Christian Dictionary to be printed were the title-page and the preliminaries. During the printing, two adjacent types in the last page of the preface were damaged. When the types from that page had been put back into the case, they were among the first to be picked up when the case was next used. Both damaged types make their first appearance in the Folio in page 45 of the Comedies.

Using evidence of this kind, Hinman was able to reconstruct not only the relationships between the Folio and Jaggard's other books, but also the order in which the pages of the Folio itself were printed.

Towards the end of the Comedies, the Folio workmen suddenly jumped ahead to the Histories, and set the first 24 pages of King John before finishing All's Well and setting Twelfth Night. Vincent's Discoverie of Errours was meanwhile nearing completion, and the first four pages of Jaggard's open letter to 'Master York' (Ralph Brooke, York Herald) had been printed. Most of the final page of that letter was set with type distributed from page 23 of King John, but it was not printed immediately. The final paragraph—perhaps a revised version substituted at the last minute—contains several types distributed from a page of Twelfth Night.

Shown below are two extracts from page 267 of the Folio Comedies, each containing two of the types in question, and the final paragraph of Jaggard's letter in which all four types reappear.

Twelfe Night, or

You should finde better dealing what's to do?
Shall we go see the reliques of this Towne?
Ant. To morrow sir, best first go see your Lodging?
Seb. I am not weary, and 'tis long to night

tricke of singularity : and consequently setts downe the manner how : as a sad face, a reuerend carriage, a slow tongue, in the habite of some Sir of note, and so foorth. I haue lymde her, but it is Ioues doing, and Ioue make me thankefull. And when she went away now, let this Fellow be look'd too : Fellow? not *Maluolio,* nor after my degree, but Fellow. Why euery thing adheres togither, that no dramme of a scruple, no scruple of a scruple, no

What satisfaction a Partiall Reader may receyue by this my iust Apologie, I know not; but howsoeuer, it is enough for me, that I haue satisfied my selfe in it, that M. *Yorke* may vnderstand, it touches a Printer as much to maintaine his reputation in the Art he liues by, as a Herald in his Profession, and that if any affront be done me in that kinde, I shall be euer as sensible of it, as hee would be of the like done to himselfe : howsoeuer it hath pleased God to make me, and him to style me a Blinde-Printer, though I could tell him by the way, that it is no right conclusion in schooles, that because *Homer was Blinde and a Poet,* therefore hee was a Blinde-Poet.   FAREWELL.

three folios were usually in progress at the same time (Vincent, Shakespeare, and Favyn). In the summer, however, both Shakespeare and Favyn (though probably not Vincent) were interrupted by yet another book. William Burton's *Description of Leicestershire* was apparently printed from start to finish between mid-July and late October 1622. After Vincent's *Discoverie* was finished in December, the next 12 months were spent mainly on Shakespeare and Favyn, with occasional interruptions by small pieces of job-printing (including a cancel leaf that corrected an error in Burton's *Leicestershire*). Neither the First Folio nor Favyn's *Theater of Honour* was quite finished when William Jaggard died in October 1623.

Before the relationships between the Folio and the other books of 1622 were explored, it was thought that William and Isaac Jaggard originally intended to finish printing the Folio before 1623. The twice-yearly catalogue of books exhibited at the Frankfurt Fair did not include English books, but in 1622 the English reprints of that catalogue began to include a supplement of English titles. The list of books ostensibly printed in April–October 1622 includes Vincent's *Discoverie*, Favyn's *Theater*, and 'Playes, written by M. *William Shakespeare*, all in one volume, printed by *Isaack Iaggard*, in fol.' It is, however, unrealistic to deduce that the Jaggards

A different kind of link between the Folio and another book was recently found on the page reproduced above, in a 'made-up' copy of Richard II *and* Henry IV *assembled from odd leaves taken from several dismembered Folios.*

A proof copy of page 413 of Favyn's Theater *was apparently printed while the ink of page 414 was still very wet. In the lower half of page 413, which is blank, the paper came under comparatively little pressure, but in the upper half the pressure was enough to set off the wet ink of page 414 on the tympan cloth of the press. Before that ink was dry, the same press began to print pages 42–3 of the Histories, and the tympan cloth left clear traces of Favyn page 414 on the first two or three copies of page 42 (in the original, the weave of the cloth is clearly visible).*

In Folger copy 65, similar but fainter traces of another page of Favyn's Theater *have been found on page 163 of the Histories.*

either planned or hoped to finish the Folio before the end of 1622, let alone by October. No matter when they submitted the entries for inclusion in the *Catalogus Universalis*, they were far too experienced to imagine that more than one of the three books could be finished by October, even without possible interruptions by other books such as Burton's *Leicestershire*. (In fact, the only one completed before the *following* October was Vincent's *Discoverie*.) What the *Catalogus* entries show is that all three books were in progress by mid-1622, and were being advertised as forthcoming.

A CATALOGVE OF SVCH BOOKES AS HAVE beene published, and (by authoritie) printed in *English*, since the last Vernall *Mart*, which was in *Aprill* 1622. till this present *October* 1622.

He History of the life and reigne of King *Henry* the seuenth, written by the Right Honourable *Francis* Lord Verulam Viscount Saint Albons. The second Edition. Printed for *Matthew Lownes* and *William Barret*, in fol.

The Imperiall history, Or a true relation of the liues and reignes of all the Roman Emperors, from the time of *Iulius Cesar*, first founder of the Roman Empire and Monarchy, to *Ferdinand* the second now reigning, printed for *Mat. Lownes* in fol.

A Discouery of Errors in *Yorkes* Catalogue of Nobilitie, published 1619 with a reuiew of his second Edition thereof, together with the seuerall successions and new creations, to this present yeere 1622. by *Augustine Vincent*, Rougecrom Pursiuant of Armes, printed by *William Iaggard* in fol.

Playes, written by M. *William Shakespeare*, all in one volume, printed by *Isaack Iaggard*, in fol.

The Theater of Honor and Knighthood, printed by *William Iaggard*, in fol.

Despite the heading of the supplement to the London edition of the Catalogus Universalis *for Autumn 1622, the Jaggards cannot have expected more than one of the three books they listed in that issue to have been finished before 1623. (Bodleian Library, Oxford: reproduced by permission of the Curators.)*

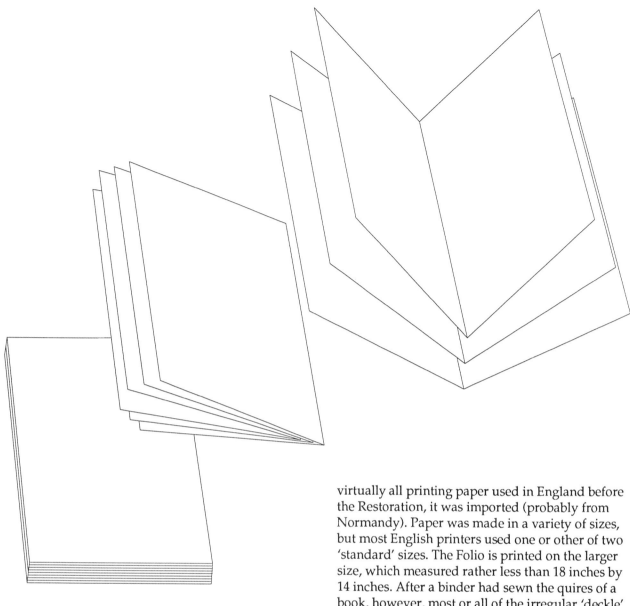

THE STRUCTURE OF THE BOOK

The Shakespeare First Folio is what is known as a 'folio in sixes'. What that means is a book made up of six-leaf sections (or 'quires'), each consisting of three sheets of paper folded together (and eventually sewn) as shown in the diagram above. Each sheet has two pages printed on each side, so each quire contains twelve pages of text (approximately half an average play). There are, in fact, a number of 'irregular' sections in the Folio. One quire has eight leaves, another has four, three have only two, and four leaves are inserted singly. Most of the quires, however, have six leaves, and most of the exceptions are consequences of (and evidence for) irregularities in the progress of the printing.

The paper is of medium quality. Like all paper of the period it is hand-made rag paper, and like virtually all printing paper used in England before the Restoration, it was imported (probably from Normandy). Paper was made in a variety of sizes, but most English printers used one or other of two 'standard' sizes. The Folio is printed on the larger size, which measured rather less than 18 inches by 14 inches. After a binder had sewn the quires of a book, however, most or all of the irregular 'deckle' edges of the leaves were usually trimmed off, and no completely uncut copy of the Folio survives. The pages in the few largest copies measure about 13½ by 8¾ inches. Most copies, however, are at least half an inch shorter and narrower, while some that have been rebound more than once have lost even more of their margins. In some cases, box-rules and even parts of the text have been cut away.

COMPOSITORS AND SPELLINGS

The type for the book was set by hand, and most quires are the work of more than one compositor. In 1919, Thomas Satchell noticed that while a number of common words were spelled one way in the first half of *Macbeth*, in the rest of the play they were spelled differently. Although he recognized that the printed text might simply reflect the spelling habits of two scribes who had copied out the manuscript, Satchell suggested that the different preferences more probably belonged to two compositors.

Before the eighteenth century, few English words had a single, standard, 'correct' spelling. It is not strictly true that *any* spelling was acceptable: when Shakespeare wrote Hamlet's dying words, he might have written that the rest was either *sylence* or *scilens*, but a spelling such as *cyghlunse* would have been as 'wrong' then as now. Words such as *and*, *but*, and *for* rarely had more than three letters; *thee* was acceptable with only one *e*, but *the* was almost never written with two.

By 1600 the spelling of printed books had become noticeably more consistent than that of manuscripts. It has sometimes been suggested that regional variety was simply being stifled by the local habits of a monopolistic London book trade. The real explanation is more down to earth: no matter where a compositor came from, consistent spelling was a matter of practical convenience. It was customary for each compositor to distribute the same pages that he had set. If he did so carelessly, and dropped too many types into the wrong compartments of the type-case, the number of misprints in his next pages would increase. It would eventually become necessary to sort out all the types in the case—a lengthy and tedious job that had to be done in the compositor's own time.

If a compositor habitually spelled *do* with only two letters, a single glance at the word while distributing would tell him that his hand needed to pause once over the 'd' box, once over the 'o' box, and once over the space box. If, however, he used the forms *do*, *doe*, and *doo* interchangeably and at random, when distributing he would have to memorize each successive spelling. If he thought only of the word, he would run the risk of dropping an 'e' or an 'o' into the space box or vice versa. Quite simply, consistent spelling meant faster and more accurate distribution.

Satchell's suggestion about the spellings in *Macbeth* prompted others to investigate further. The most easily observed difference between the two groups of habits was that while 'Compositor A' preferred the spellings *doe*, *goe*, and *here*, 'Compositor B' preferred *do*, *go*, and *heere*. Neither of the workmen was absolutely consistent—especially in prose and long lines of verse, where altering spellings was a common way of adjusting the length of a line. But most pages in the Folio showed signs of a bias towards one group of habits or the other, and by the 1950s almost all the pages had been attributed more or less confidently to either Compositor A or Compositor B. In some pages the evidence was confusingly mixed, and some scholars suggested that those pages might be the work of a

The passage above, from 3 Henry VI (Histories, page 159), *was set by Compositor A, and shows a cluster of his characteristic* doe *spellings. Neither* goe *nor* here *is illustrated (neither word is used as often as* do*), but A's preference for using an 'a' in* deare *or* dearely *is also shown.*

third compositor. Many, however, considered that three compositors in a single book was rather unlikely, and ingeniously explained that while a compositor would impose his own spellings when his copy was easy to read, he might be more likely to reproduce the spellings of less legible copy.

Hinman's reconstruction of the printing, however, showed that most of the Folio pages had been set in pairs by two compositors working simultaneously, each from a different type-case. Many of those pairs, moreover, consisted of two pages previously attributed to a single compositor, because the simple *do-go-here* test was unable to distinguish between them. Hinman's more careful study of spellings revealed that the Folio was the work of at least five compositors. Compositors B and E shared a preference for *do*, *go*, and *heere*, but differed in other respects; A and D preferred *doe*, *goe*, and *here*, though D's preferences were less consistent than A's; C preferred the longer spellings of all three words, namely *doe*, *goe*, and *heere*. Later studies divided Hinman's 'A' into A and F, bringing the number to six, and it has since been plausibly suggested that the remaining 'A' pages may include the work of at least three other compositors. Where once there were 'two', there now appear to have been at least nine compositors.

Prouoke vs hither now, to flaughter thee.

Cla. If you do loue my Brother, hate not me:
I am his Brother, and I loue him well.
If you are hyr'd for meed, go backe againe,
And I will fend you to my Brother Gloufter:
Who fhall reward you better for my life,
Then *Edward* will for tydings of my death.

   2 You are decciu'd,
Your Brother Gloufter hates you.

  Cla. Oh no, he loues me, and he holds me deere:
Go you to him from me.

   1 I fo we will.

  Cla. Tell him, when that our Princely Father Yorke,
Bleft his three Sonnes with his victorious Arme,
He little thought of this diuided Friendfhip:
Bid Gloufter thinke on this, and he will weepe,

   1 I Milftones, as he leffoned vs to weepe.

  Cla. O do not flander him, for he is kinde,

   1 Right, as Snow in Haruest:
Come, you deceiue your felfe,
'Tis he that fends vs to deftroy you heere.

  Cla. It cannot be, for he bewept my Fortune,

This passage, from Richard III *(Histories, page 181), was set by Compositor B, and includes four of his best-documented preferential spellings:* do, go, heere, *and* deere.

THE IMPORTANCE OF COMPOSITOR B

The compositor known as B set nearly half the pages in the book—more than twice as many as any other compositor. His work has also been identified in other Jaggard books as far back as 1619, so it is safe to assume that he was a 'resident' employee. He was probably one of the journeymen named in William Jaggard's will, all of whom were former Jaggard apprentices, but we do not know which one he might have been. (One John Shakespeare—no relation—served his apprenticeship with Jaggard in 1610–17, but he is not mentioned in the will, and probably worked elsewhere after serving out his term.) The fact that B set so much of the Folio may suggest that he was given special responsibility for that book, while another of the 'regular' compositors similarly took charge of the work on Favyn's *Theater of Honour*. If so, that compositor was probably either A or C, because none of the others is very likely to have been a full-time employee.

Because he set so many Folio pages, Compositor B's work can be studied in depth. It is possible to examine his work in plays that were simply reprinted from earlier quartos, and to analyze the ways in which he treated the text. In pages set from printed copy, it is possible to see not only how he 'modernized' the punctuation and spelling of the copy, but also the kind of mistakes he was most likely to make, and how often he made them. That information can then be applied to plays that appeared for the first time in the Folio. Where there appears to be an error, a detailed knowledge of the compositor's habits can make it easier to diagnose the probable *cause* of the error—and that can make it easier to deduce what the reading should really have been.

The other compositors can be studied in the same way, but none of them set nearly as many pages from printed copy as did Compositor B, and some worked only from manuscripts. There is consequently less evidence from which to analyze their characteristics. If their work can be found in other books, their performance when setting from printed copy can be studied more closely. But they may be difficult to identify in other books without equally careful reconstructions of the typesetting, and they were not all regular Jaggard employees.

THE TEENAGE APPRENTICE

Compositor B's role in the printing of the Folio apparently extended beyond those pages that he set himself, because he seems also to have taken the overall responsibility for the work of another compositor. The pages set by Compositor E are confined to the Tragedies and the last of the Histories, so he cannot have started working on the Folio before March or April 1623. One of his most striking characteristics is his extreme lack of skill: errors of every kind are far more frequent in his pages than in any others. Even in his earliest work, many of his spelling habits resemble those of Compositor B (with whom he almost invariably worked), but when his pages are examined in chronological order it can be seen that his habits become more and more like those of his partner as the work progresses. It seems fairly obvious that he was an apprentice whose training was being supervised by Compositor B.

On 8 November 1622 William Jaggard took on the first apprentice he had bound since 1614. There can be little doubt that Compositor E was that same apprentice: John Leason, the son of a yeoman of Husley, Hampshire. His articles of indenture specified that he should serve for seven years—the statutory minimum term for an apprenticeship. According to a City regulation, no apprentice could be freed before his 24th birthday, so Leason must have been at least 17 years old when he began to work on the Folio. It is unlikely that he was much older.

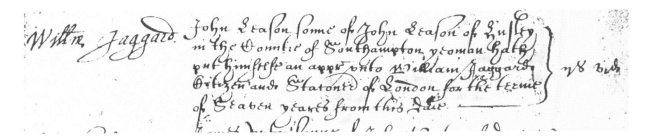

This entry in the Register of Apprentices records the binding of William Jaggard's last apprentice (probably Compositor E) on 8 November 1622. The apprentice is named as 'John Leason sonne of John Leason of Husley in the Countie of Southampton, yeoman'. (Stationers' Hall: reproduced by permission of the Master and Wardens of the Worshipful Company of Stationers and Newspaper Makers.)

THE ORDER OF THE PAGES

Before Hinman's study was published, it had usually been taken for granted that the text of each play had been printed from beginning to end in the 'obvious' order. Such, however, was not the case. The 12 pages in each quire are arranged in pairs on the three sheets as shown below. If the pages had been set in numerical order, the press could not have started printing any of them until the first complete pair—pages 6 and 7—had been finished. In addition to causing long delays, that system would have required a very large stock of type. No page could be distributed before pages 6 and 7 had been printed—so unless the compositors stopped work while the press was in use, they would have needed enough additional type to keep them busy until pages 6 and 7 could be distributed. Like most printers in Jacobean London, Jaggard simply did not own enough type to set eight or nine Folio pages. He therefore followed the common English practice known as 'setting by formes' (a 'forme' is a group of type-pages to be printed on one side of a sheet).

The usual method of setting a Folio quire was to begin by estimating how much text would fit in the first five pages—a process known as 'casting off' the copy. Pages 6 and 7 were the first to be set, sometimes by two men working simultaneously, but more usually by a single compositor. When those two pages (the first forme) had been made ready and given to the press, pages 5 and 8 (the next forme) were set. Those two pages were far enough apart for the copy to be physically divided between two compositors, so they were usually set by two men working simultaneously. While the press printed pages 5 and 8, the compositors distributed pages 6 and 7, and then set pages 4 and 9. After another distribution they set pages 3 and 10, then pages 2 and 11, and finally pages 1 and 12. So although the last seven pages of each quire were set in numerical order, the first five pages were set in *reverse* order.

THE IMPORTANCE OF CASTING OFF

It was not always easy to cast off manuscript copy accurately. Once pages 6 and 7 had been printed, the text assigned to pages 1–5 *had* to be fitted into those pages. If the contents of page 5 had been carelessly calculated, the compositor had a choice. He could try to follow the casting-off mark exactly, by squeezing in extra lines or by spacing out the text as appropriate. Alternatively, he could put off the problem by ignoring the mark—he could set in the usual way, make up page 5 when he had set the right number of lines, and then make a new

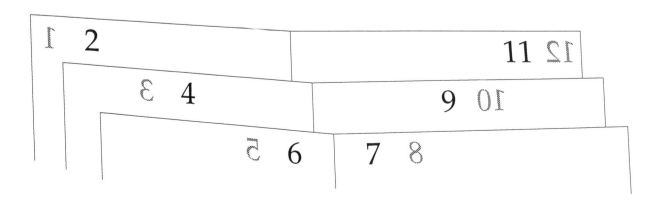

mark of his own in the copy to show where the page had *really* started. If he then did the same with pages 4 and 3 and 2, when the time came to fit what remained into page 1, he might well find himself in difficulties.

The scene-heading shown below is a 'normal' one from a page in the second half of quire nn of Hamlet *(Tragedies, page 155).*

Till then fit ftill my foule; foule deeds will rife,
Though all the earth orewhelm them to mens eies. *Exit.*

Scena Tertia.

Enter Laertes and Ophelia.
Laer. My neceffaries are imbark't; Farewell:

The example below is from the first page of quire Aa in The Winter's Tale *(Comedies, page 277). A miscalculation in casting off left the compositor with too much text to fit the page, so he gained extra space by omitting all four white lines from the scene-heading.*

Arch. If the King had no Sonne, they would defire to liue on Crutches till he had one. *Exeunt.*

Scæna Secunda.

Enter Leontes, Hermione, Mamillius, Polixenes, Camillo.
Pol. Nine Changes of the Watry-Starre hath been

The example below is from the first page of quire ss in King Lear *(Tragedies, page 305), and shows the opposite problem. The compositor did not have enough text to fill the page in the normal way, so he had to find ways of spacing it out. His methods included using a white line below the opening stage direction of this scene and setting the first two lines of verse as four half-lines.*

Farre off methinkes I heare the beaten Drumme.
Come Father, Ile beftow you with a Friend. *Exeunt.*

Scæna Septima.

Enter Cordelia, Kent, and Gentleman.

Cor. O thou good *Kent,*
How fhall I liue and worke
To match thy goodneffe?
My life will be too fhort,
And euery meafure faile me.
Kent. To be acknowledg'd Madam is ore-paid

There were several easy ways of making minor adjustments. A stage direction could be set with or without a 'white line' (a line of spaces) above it, or with another below it. Both above and below a scene-heading, there was usually a pair of white lines separated by a rule, so one or more of the white lines could be omitted if necessary. Exits were usually set against the right margin. If there was room, an exit could occupy a line by itself; if not, it could share a line with the end of a speech. If there was still a problem, verse could either be run together as prose or chopped into half-lines.

Sometimes, however, the measures adopted were even more extreme. *Much Ado About Nothing* ends on the first page of quire L, and whoever did the casting off left rather too much text to be crammed into that page. In this case the Folio text can be compared with the Quarto of 1600, from which it was set. Among the inevitable crop of misprints in the Folio page, one whole line of text is omitted. That omission may have been accidental, but the line was 'Heere comes the Prince and Claudio', spoken immediately before a stage direction for the entrance of those characters. A compositor in search of extra space might well have decided that the line could be sacrificed without substantial loss.

In *Antony and Cleopatra*, the first page of quire zz (Tragedies, page 365) is another in which the text fits rather tightly. In that page the lines spoken by Proculeius immediately before and after Cleopatra is captured are printed as two consecutive speeches, each with the speech-heading, '*Pro.*' It is possible that nothing has been omitted. If the speech was divided between pages of the manuscript, the '*Pro.*' heading may have been repeated at the beginning of the new page. More probably, however, a stage direction describing Cleopatra's capture has been left out. That may be all—but the half-line spoken immediately before the capture is followed by a complete line when Proculeius resumes. It is therefore possible that at least one speech (perhaps a half-line spoken by Cleopatra) has also been omitted for lack of space.

By contrast, the first two pages of quire ss in *King Lear* (Tragedies, pp. 305–6) contain far less text than normal, and some lines of verse had to be broken into half-lines for the sake of filling space. The Folio text of *Lear* differs substantially from the Quarto of 1608, and the differences include numerous short insertions, one of which is found in the second column of page 305. Where the Quarto had a single verse line ('Fourescore and vpward, and to deale plainely'), the Folio has three lines of type. The Quarto line has been cut in two, and 'Not an houre more, nor lesse:' has been inserted between the two half-lines.

> *Cla.* I had well hop'd y̅ wouldſt haue denied *Beatrice,*y̅
> I might haue cudgel'd thee out of thy ſingle life,to make
> thee a double dealer, which out of queſtiõ thou wilt be,
> if my Couſin do not looke exceeding narrowly to thee.
>   *Bene.* Come,come, we are friends, let's haue a dance
> ere we are married,that we may lighten our own hearts,
> and our wiues heeles.
>   *Leon.* Wee'll haue dancing afterward.
>   *Bene.* Firſt,of my vvord,therfore play muſick.*Prince,*
> thou art ſad,get thee a vvife,get thee a vvife, there is no
> ſtaff more reuerend then one tipt with horn. *Enter. Meſ.*
>   *Meſſen.* My Lord,your brother *Iohn* is tane in flight,
> And brought with armed men backe to *Meſſina.*
>   *Bene.* Thinke not on him till to morrow , ile deuiſe
> thee braue puniſhments for him: ſtrike vp Pipers.*Dance.*
>   L   *F I N I S.*

Shown here is one of the most obviously crowded passages in the Folio: the end of Much Ado about Nothing, *on the first page of quire L (Comedies, page 121). Among other expedients, the compositor resorted to using contractions in the first and third lines. (As is the case when* the *is contracted to* ye, *the* y *element in the first two contractions stands for* th. *The contracted words are* thou *and* that.) *He also squeezed the Messenger's entrance into the end of a line, and put 'FINIS' into the 'direction line' below the text. (The L in that line is the 'signature' identifying quire L.)*

'Fourscore and upward' means 'over eighty'. It is anyway inappropriate to define an indefinite number of years to the nearest hour—but while 'not an hour less' makes a kind of sense, 'not an hour *more* than over eighty' makes none at all. The substance gains little from the addition, and the disrupted verse gains even less—but the line does help to fill the page. As 'evidence', that is at best only circumstantial—but it is not unreasonable to suspect that the line *may* have been made up in the printing house for the sole purpose of filling space.

STOP-PRESS CORRECTIONS

Few copies of the Folio are textually identical. On more than 100 occasions, the press was stopped so that corrections could be made to one or both of the pages then being printed. The sheets printed before correction—often relatively few, but sometimes more than half the heap—were neither thrown away nor set aside as 'seconds'. When the whole heap of sheets had been printed, the uncorrected copies were together at the bottom, but the

One of the most notable variants in the whole Folio is found in the final scene of Richard II *(Histories, page 45). The uncorrected state 1 is here reproduced from Folger copy 35 (the only recorded copy), and the corrected state 2 is shown on the facing page. A two-line speech is missing from state 1 near the top of the second column. In state 2 the speech has been inserted, and what were previously the first two lines of the column have been moved back into column 1.*

The reason why two lines had to be moved back was that column 2 was unprecedentedly full: unlike any previous part-page, it had no white line between the final line and the rule below. The reason why the lines could be moved back so easily was that column 1 contained no fewer than five white lines, two of them redundant. One of the five was in the 'expected' position at the end of the column, and two were outside the rules of the scene-heading. But although there were no white lines inside those rules, there was one above an entrance in the previous scene, and another below the entrance here illustrated.

The unequal spacing, and the fact that in state 1 this is the only page in the book in which the columns of text differ in length, suggest that even the 'uncorrected' state incorporates changes made after the page was first set. Those changes probably included inserting at least one line in column 2, and removing at least two from column 1.

It is likely, indeed, that the speech inserted in the corrected state of column 2 was originally misplaced in column 1, and that the first proof indicated that it should be moved. Because there was another insertion in column 2, the compositor misunderstood the instructions, removed the speech entirely, and 'padded' column 1 with extra white lines rather than equalizing the columns. When the printing began, an early copy was checked against the first proof, and the mistake was noticed and corrected.

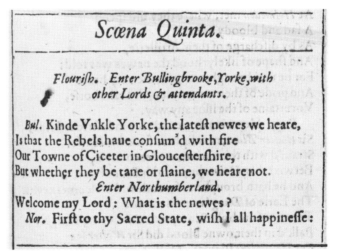

> ### Scœna Quinta.
>
> *Flouriſh. Enter Bullingbrooke,Yorke,with*
> *other Lords & attendants.*
>
> *Bul.* Kinde Vnkle Yorke, the lateſt newes we heare,
> Is that the Rebels haue conſum'd with fire
> Our Towne of Ciceter in Glouceſterſhire,
> But whether they be tane or ſlaine, we heare not.
>   *Enter Northumberland.*
> Welcome my Lord : What is the newes ?
>   *Nor.* Firſt to thy Sacred State, wiſh I all happineſſe:

> ### Richard the Second.   45
>
> The next newes is, I haue to London ſent
> The heads of *Salsbury,Spencer,Blunt,*and *Kent* :
> The manner of their taking may appeare
> At large diſcourſed in this paper heere.
>   *Enter Fitz-waters.*

heap was then separated into small sheaves of no more than a few sheets, folded, and hung up on lines to dry. By the time the dry sheets had been taken down and stacked, the heap had often been effectively shuffled. When copies of the finished book were assembled, most of them included at least a few of the variant pages in the uncorrected state. No known copy has all those pages in the final state; none has so many in the earliest state that it can be called an early *copy*. Furthermore, no two copies have yet been found to contain exactly the same mixture of early and late pages.

The Folio is by no means unusual in this respect. Virtually all English books printed before the eighteenth century vary to some extent from copy to copy, although few other books have been so thoroughly searched for variants. As in most books, the majority of the variants found in the Folio are fairly trivial: corrections of obvious misprints such as inverted letters and wrong page-numbers, and changes in spacing, spelling, and punctuation. Most of the alterations could have been made simply by taking one of the first sheets off the press and looking for obvious ways to improve it. That, indeed, was probably how most of the changes *were* made, because very few of them suggest that the printed sheet had been reread against the copy from which it had been set.

Most of the known variants were found by Hinman during his page-by-page comparison of

55 Folger copies. At the time he undertook that study, it was still widely believed that when corrections were made during the press-run, they were the only corrections made at all. The very fact that there *were* errors in the text when the printing began was taken as evidence that there had been no prior proofreading. That theory was rarely accepted by scholars who had any practical experience of hand-press printing, but Hinman himself had not yet begun to question it when his book was published. Ironically, some of the best evidence for an earlier stage of correction had been found by Hinman's own investigation of the printing order. Distinctive types sometimes reappear in pages set before those types could have been distributed. In some cases the only plausible explanation is that the type was inserted *after* the page was originally set—in other words, during correction. Furthermore, some of the errors found in 'uncorrected' states of variant pages can only be adequately explained as miscorrections of earlier mistakes. A good example is the variant passage shown at the foot of the preceding columns.

Every page of the Folio was probably read against the copy at least once before printing—but probably *only* once. As the players were cooperating in the venture, some of the early pages may have been sent out to be proofed in the playhouse. It would, however, have been more efficient to have given the job to a printing-house employee, who would be available whenever a forme was ready to be proofed. The correction was probably hasty and (by modern standards) inadequate. Many errors were certainly overlooked, and some of them are obvious—in pages in which others (perhaps once even more obvious) have already been corrected. But although some scholars still believe otherwise, there are no reasonable grounds for doubting that the text of the Folio was proofed before the printing began.

The usual purpose of a second inspection was to check whether the corrections marked on the first proof had been carried out. Sometimes the reader would have found one or two that had been overlooked; sometimes he would have found errors that he had failed to notice before. In the Comedies and Histories, only about one page in 14 was checked, but in the Tragedies the rate jumped to more than one in six. The reason was simple: Compositor E was not only unskilled at setting type, but was also particularly prone to make new mistakes while correcting. More than half the pages he set and corrected were checked again at press. Even at that stage he could make matters worse. On several occasions he inserted the right letter in the wrong place, and once he made a perfect correction to the wrong word.

Scæna Quinta.

Flourish. Enter Bullingbrooke, Yorke, with other Lords & attendants.
Bul. Kinde Vnkle Yorke, the latest newes we heare,
Is that the Rebels haue consum'd with fire
Our Towne of Ciceter in Gloucestershire,
But whether they be tane or slaine, we heare not.
Enter Northumberland.
Welcome my Lord: What is the newes?
Nor. First to thy Sacred State, wish I all happinesse:
The next newes is, I haue to London sent
The heads of *Salsbury, Spencer, Blunt,* and *Kent:*

Richard the Second.   45

The manner of their taking may appeare
At large discoursed in this paper heere.
    Bul. We thank thee gentle *Percy* for thy paines,
And to thy worth will adde right worthy gaines.
            Enter Fitz-waters.

Surviving proofsheets

Proofsheets that were printed and marked for the first stage of correction were usually discarded. Like the errors they corrected, they were meant to be disposed of, and very few examples have survived. The status of a sheet marked for correction during the press-run, however, was different. Some copies of the book would anyway contain the uncorrected readings—so although the marked proof was not as good as a printed copy of the corrected state, it was better than a completely uncorrected sheet. Sometimes, then, the sheet marked by the corrector was put back into the heap of printed sheets, and was eventually bound into a copy of the finished book. There was no reason to suppose that the purchaser would object to finding a few manuscript corrections in a new book—in some books of the day, belated corrections were made by pen in *all* copies.

Marked proofsheets of that kind have been noticed in dozens of early books. No fewer than five have been found in copies of the First Folio (extracts from three are illustrated below), and more may yet be discovered. All five have been found in the Tragedies, and in each example, corrections are marked in only one page. All five of those pages were set by Compositor E.

Folger copy 48 contains the proofsheet that was marked for the correction of a page of King Lear *(Tragedies, page 292). The correction shown is an instruction to delete the second l in holly (a mistake for holy). Having removed the l, the compositor had to put in an extra space to fill the line. He inserted it after cords, but failed to push it down far enough to prevent it from being inked and partly printed (see facing page).*

Folger copy 47 contains the proofsheet that was marked for the correction of a page of Othello *(Tragedies, page 333). In the extract shown, the first two corrections indicate that an inking space after singing should be pushed down, and that i should be deleted to correct* neither *to* nether *(see facing page). In the third of the corrected lines, a binder has cut away the marginal a and g that once completed the instructions on how to correct* Sonle set sining.

The best-known Folio proofsheet was marked for the correction of a page of Antony and Cleopatra *(Tragedies, page 352). The leaf was found in a bookseller's collection of unbound leaves by J. O. Halliwell-Phillipps over a century ago. Note that in the last corrected line, the corrections are marked in the 'wrong' order. The corrector first decided that* rume *needed to be altered to* rheume, *and only then decided which two letters would have to be deleted to make enough space for the lengthened word.*

NEGOTIATIONS WITH OTHER PUBLISHERS

By the summer of 1623, the work was nearing completion. For some reason, Blount and Jaggard had not taken the trouble to acquire all the existing publication rights before the printing began, but most of the belated negotiations had been successful. William Aspley (who owned two plays) and John Smethwick (who owned four, including the earlier *Taming of a Shrew*) had chosen to become shareholders in the venture rather than to lease or sell their rights. Thomas Pavier had transferred all his rights except those to *Pericles* (excluded from the Folio for reasons unknown), and he may well

You beaftly knaue,know you no reuerence?
Kent. Yes Sir,but anger hath a priuiledge.
Cor. Why art thou angrie?
Kent. That fuch a flaue as this fhould weare a Sword,
Who weares no honefty : fuch fmiling rogues as thefe,
Like Rats oft bite the holy cords¹ a twaine,
Which are t'intrince, t'vnloofe : fmooth euery paffion
That in the natures of their Lords rebell,
Being oile to fire,fnow to the colder moodes,
Reuenge,affirme,and turne their Halcion beakes
With euery gall,and varry of their Mafters.

An old thing 'twas : but it exprefs'd her Fortune,
And fhe dy'd finging it. That Song to night,
Will not go from my mind : I haue much to do,
But to go hang my head all at one fide
And fing it like poore *Brabarie*: prythee difpatch.
Æmi. Shall I go fetch your Night-gowne?
Def. No,vn-pin me here,
This *Lodouico* is a proper man.
Æmil. A very handfome man.
Def. He fpeakes well.
Æmil. I know a Lady in Venice would haue walk'd barefoot to Paleftine for a touch of his nether lip.
Def. The poore Soule fat finging,by a Sicamour tree.
Sing all a greene Willough :

The Swannes downe feather
That ftands vpon the Swell at the full of Tide:
And neither way inclines.
Eno. Will *Cæfar* weepe?
Agr. He ha's a cloud in's face.
Eno. He were the worfe for that were he a Horfe,fo is he being a man.
Agri. Why *Enobarbus* :
When *Anthony* found *Iulius Cæfar* dead,
He cried almoft to roaring : And he wept,
When at Phillippi he found *Brutus* flaine.
Eno. That yeare indeed,he was trobled with a rheume,
What willingly he did confound,he wail'd,

have helped to arrange deals with Arthur Johnson (*The Merry Wives of Windsor*) and Nathaniel Butter (*King Lear*). When William Jaggard drew up his will in March 1623, his wife and his friend Pavier were named as joint executors.

Another publisher, however, had apparently been less cooperative. Work on the Histories had begun during an interruption in the progress of the Comedies, perhaps because the manuscript of *Twelfth Night* was temporarily unavailable. After part of *Richard II* had been set, the Comedies were completed—but instead of returning to *Richard II*, the compositors skipped the rest of that play and both parts of *Henry IV*, and began to set *Henry V*.

The most likely explanation is that Blount and Isaac Jaggard waited until the Histories were in progress before negotiating with Matthew Law, who owned *Richard II*, both *Henry IV* plays, and *Richard III*. The second part of *Henry IV* had not sold well, but the others were the three best-selling Shakespeare plays, and Law was in a position to drive a hard bargain. Terms were apparently not agreed until the compositors had nearly reached *Richard III*. Before continuing, they went back and set the omitted plays first.

TROUBLE WITH *TROILUS*

A more serious problem, however, arose in the Tragedies. As the order of plays was originally planned, *Romeo and Juliet* should have been followed by *Troilus and Cressida*, the rights to which belonged to Henry Walley—but Walley evidently decided otherwise. The 1609 Quarto had probably not sold particularly well, and Walley may have refused to allow the play to be reprinted while much of his own edition remained unsold.

After setting one and a half sheets of the quire in which *Romeo* ended and *Troilus* began, the compositors left the second sheet unfinished. Henry Walley's decision must have seemed final, because the work on *Troilus* was not merely postponed—it was abandoned. Four of the five remaining pages of *Romeo* were printed on a single sheet as a four-page quire, pending a decision about what to print on the back of the fifth and last page. That decision was made a few weeks later, and *Timon of Athens* was set to fill the place once intended for *Troilus*. Perhaps *Timon* would otherwise have appeared later in the book—but it is possible that if *Troilus* had not been abandoned, *Timon* might never have been printed at all. The rest of the book was then 'completed' on the assumption that *Troilus* could not be included. As will be explained below, it was not in fact included until after the first few copies of the volume had been sold without it.

THE DEATH OF WILLIAM JAGGARD

William Jaggard, who had made his will on 28 March, died sometime before 4 November 1623 (when Isaac was formally appointed Printer to the City of London in his place). He may or may not have still been alive when the final page of *Cymbeline* (the last play in the volume) was printed. The page ends with a statement that the book was printed *'at the charges of W. Iaggard'* and others, but that was no less true after his death. We cannot date either event very precisely, but by the end of October 1623, Jaggard had died and *Cymbeline* had been completed. So far as the publishers knew, all that remained to be printed after *Cymbeline* were the preliminaries—the title, dedication, preface, commendatory verses, and list of contents. As luck would have it, they were wrong.

THE PORTRAIT OF SHAKESPEARE

The engraved portrait on the Folio title-page was not printed on the same press that printed the text. The letter on a printing type stands out in relief, and the ink on the raised surface is printed by pressing the paper vertically down on it. The lines of an engraving, on the other hand, are cut into a copper plate. After inking, the surface of the plate is wiped clean, and the ink remaining in the cuts is then printed by forcing the plate and the paper between two rollers under heavy pressure.

Unlike some London printers, Jaggard may have had a rolling press of his own. But the Folio title-page was printed on a separate leaf rather than as part of a quire, which suggests that the portrait may have been printed elsewhere by a rolling press specialist. If so, the most likely candidate is the engraver himself, Martin Droeshout.

Like many pages in the text, the portrait is variant. In the first few copies printed, there is so little shading on the ruff that Shakespeare's head seems to be floating in mid-air. The plate was therefore modified, most notably by shading an area of the ruff below Shakespeare's left ear. Not long afterwards, the plate was modified a second time, when minor changes were made to the hair and to the highlights in the eyes. It is unlikely that anyone but Droeshout would have considered those alterations necessary.

The precise date of the portrait has not been determined (it may have been printed at any time during or after 1622), but the lines of printed text on the title-page must have been added by early November 1623.

REGISTRATION AND SEARCH

On 8 November, when the preliminaries were either in progress or finished, Isaac Jaggard and Edward Blount went to Stationers' Hall to register their rights to the plays that had not been printed before. To the best of their knowledge, there were

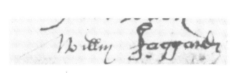
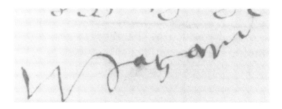

The first of the Jaggard signatures shown above was written in December 1602. (Stationers' Hall: reproduced by permission of the Master and Wardens of the Worshipful Company of Stationers and Newspaper Makers.) The second was written while the Folio Histories were being printed, when Jaggard made his will on 28 March 1623. (Guildhall Library: reproduced by permission of the Diocesan Registrar to the Bishop of London.) The reason why the two differ so strikingly is that when Jaggard signed his will, he was blind.

It was Isaac Jaggard, rather than William, who was Blount's main partner in the publication of the Folio. By the time the book appeared, Isaac had also inherited the press that actually printed it. But the colophon (printed shortly before or after William died) suggests that William Jaggard himself had invested in the publication of the Folio as well as printing it.

Printed at the Charges of W. Iaggard, Ed. Blount, I. Smithweeke, and W. Aspley, 1623.

After a few copies of the engraved portrait had been printed, the engraver made several alterations, the most obvious being the addition of a shadow between the face and the ruff. Shown above are the first state (Folger copy 2) and the second (Folger copy 1). Most copies are in the third state, printed after three almost imperceptible alterations had been made during a second interruption.

16 unregistered plays, but when they first had the titles copied into the Register (in Folio order), they prudently restricted their claim to 'soe manie of the said Copies as are not formerly entred to other men'.

An entry in the Stationers' Register served two purposes. It formally recorded the payment, to the Stationers' Company as a corporation, of a fee of sixpence for the Company's permission to print each separate work entered. By the early 1580s, such an entry had also come to serve as an official 'entry of record', or legal proof that a stationer owned the rights to a work. In that second role, the entry benefited the individual stationer rather than the Company, and the Clerk had to be paid a separate, unrecorded, personal fee of fourpence for writing it.

The exact fee owed to the Company by Blount and Jaggard could not be determined until it was known whether any of the plays had indeed been 'formerly entred'. The sum recorded beside the entry is not the 8s. payable for 16 titles, but only 7s.—and it is not written in the same ink as the entry. Blount and Jaggard must therefore have asked the Clerk to make a search. In 1623 the unit search fee was probably fourpence (again paid personally to the Clerk, and not recorded as a payment to the Wardens' Account). For a single fee, the Clerk would search the entries made during the past 12 months; searching beyond that limit

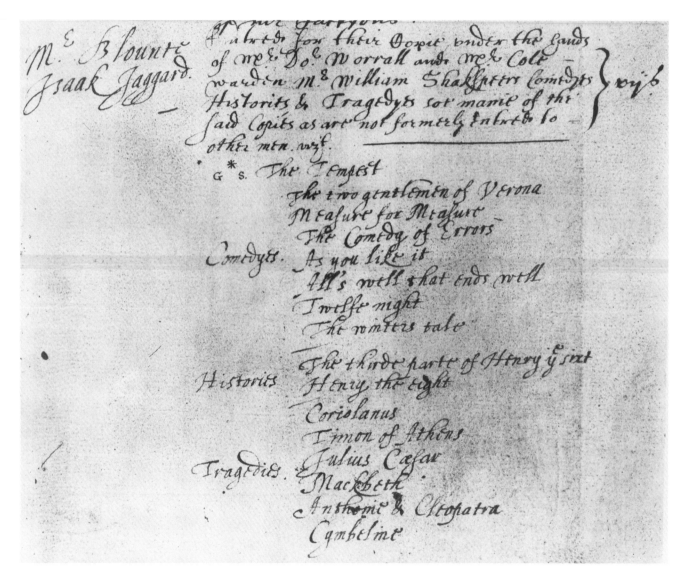

Shown above is the entry made in the Stationers' Register on 8 November 1623, listing the 16 plays that were thought not to have been entered before. The fee of seven shillings ('vij s.') was noted later, after a search revealed that each of the publishers already owned one of the plays. (Stationers' Hall: reproduced by permission of the Master and Wardens of the Worshipful Company of Stationers and Newspaper Makers.)

The letters 'G*S.' beside the first title are not part of the entry. They are the initials of George Steevens, the first editor to make a systematic search for Register entries relating to Shakespeare.

cost one additional fee for each decade searched. Four fees would have taken the search back to November 1592—but Blount and Jaggard may not have known that nothing by Shakespeare had been entered before 1593.

On a flyleaf in the Register for 1595–1620, the Clerk would have found an entry that he would have interpreted as the provisional registration of *As You Like It* by James Roberts in 1600. After Roberts retired, William Jaggard acquired most of his publishing rights, and Isaac had just inherited William's rights. Halfway through the same Register, the Clerk would have found another relevant entry, thus reducing the registration fee to 7s. for 14 plays. It is a striking testimony to the nature of Edward Blount's interest in Shakespeare's plays that although he had himself registered *Antony and Cleopatra* in 1608, by 1623 he had apparently forgotten that he owned it.

New *Troilus* negotiations

It was probably the search of the Register that led to the last-minute reinstatement of *Troilus and Cressida*. The play had been registered by Richard Bonian and Henry Walley in 1609, and had been printed for them in the same year. But when the Clerk searched the Register, he would have found that *Troilus* had been provisionally registered long before Bonian and Walley entered it—by James Roberts, in February 1603.

Sir Walter Greg suggested that the discovery of the Roberts entry would have enabled Jaggard 'to snap his fingers at Walley' and to reprint *Troilus* without further ado. That, however, is hardly likely. Roberts's entrance had been only provisional, and would have become effective only if he had 'gotten sufficient aucthority for yt'. Bonian and Walley, however, had properly obtained the authority of the deputy Master of the Revels before they registered the play, so their entrance was unconditionally valid. Furthermore, James Roberts had something of a habit of entering plays provisionally, selling them, and leaving the buyers to obtain the necessary authority. It is therefore distinctly possible that what Bonian and Walley had entered was the same manuscript, legally bought from Roberts himself.

Had the publishers simply used the Roberts entry as an excuse for defying Walley, they would have risked an immediate action for wilful and premeditated piracy, and would probably have lost. If, however, Isaac Jaggard were to have taken that entry before the Company Court, dutifully requesting a resolution of conflicting interests as Roberts's successor, the Court would undoubtedly have arbitrated one of its usual compromises. Any compromise would almost certainly have granted Isaac Jaggard the right to reprint *Troilus* at least once. What the Roberts entry would have allowed the publishers to do, therefore, was to offer Walley a choice: he could either negotiate a compromise himself or leave it to the Court.

Whatever the precise details of their new arrangement with Walley, within a few days of making the Register entry the publishers found themselves in a position to include *Troilus* after all. By then, all the rest of the Folio had been printed. The exact order in which the preliminary leaves were set is uncertain, but the sheet containing 'A Catalogue of the seuerall Comedies, Histories, and Tragedies contained in this volume' was either last or last but one. That sheet must have been printed before Henry Walley changed his mind, because the Catalogue lists only 35 plays, and does not mention *Troilus and Cressida* at all.

The belated inclusion of *Troilus*

Hinman found evidence that after the Catalogue had been printed, there was a delay (though perhaps only a short one) before the compositors began work on *Troilus*. One sheet that had been printed months earlier, containing the last page of *Romeo* and the first three of *Troilus*, still survived. The *Romeo* page could always be crossed out, so that sheet was considered usable, and the compositors began by setting the fourth page of the play. This time they worked from a manuscript rather than from the Quarto they had used before. The pages of the original sheet had been numbered 77–80; the new pages were not numbered at all, because the play was now to be inserted before the first page of the existing Tragedies.

The remaining text did not quite fit into two quires, so the final half-page had to occupy an extra leaf. If the publishers had considered the redundant page of *Romeo* to be a serious problem, it would have been easy enough to set the first page of *Troilus* again, and to print the first and last pages on the same single-sided sheet. That, however, was not done, and when the last page was printed, the Folio was once again considered to be 'complete'—for a while. After another detectable delay, somebody either noticed or remembered that the playhouse manuscript of *Troilus* contained a prologue that had not been included in the 1609 Quarto. That provided an excuse for eliminating the crossed-out page of *Romeo*. The last part of the Folio to be printed, therefore, was a single cancel leaf, with the Prologue on one side and the first page of the play reprinted on the other.

Troilus and Cressida *is not listed in the* Catalogue, *which was printed before Blount and Jaggard found it possible to include that play after all.*

The publishers originally intended that Troilus should follow Romeo and Juliet. *Before Henry Walley refused to allow the play to be included, the first three pages of* Troilus *had already been printed on a sheet that began with the last page of* Romeo.

Timon of Athens *was subsequently chosen to fill the place originally intended for* Troilus. *The last page of* Romeo *was therefore reprinted with the first page of* Timon *on the back, as shown below.*

When Troilus and Cressida *was eventually included, the publishers did not have the first three pages reprinted. They chose instead to use the original sheet, with the old final page of* Romeo *simply crossed out. A few copies of the first leaf of that sheet have survived, and both sides of it are illustrated at the top of the facing page (Folger copy 2).*

After a few copies had been sold in that form, someone suggested that the hitherto-unprinted prologue to Troilus *could be included, and so a cancel leaf was printed on which the Prologue replaced the final page of* Romeo. *The two sides of that leaf are shown at the foot of the facing page.*

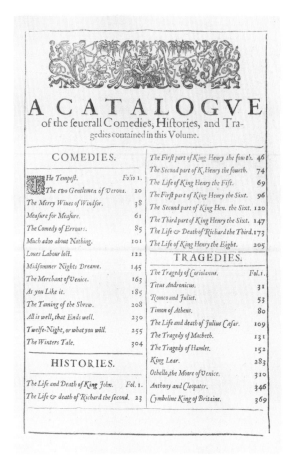

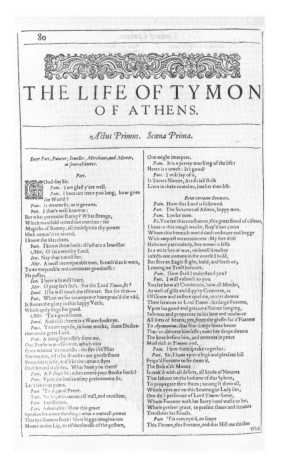

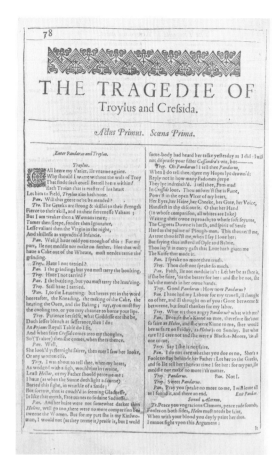

The Prologue.

IN Troy there lyes the Scene: From Iles of Greece
The Princes Orgillous, their high blood chaf'd
Haue to the Port of Athens sent their shippes
Fraught with the ministers and instruments
Of cruell Warre: Sixty and nine that wore
Their Crownets Regall, from th' Athenian bay
Put forth toward Phrygia, and their vow is made
To ransacke Troy, within whose strong emures
The rauish'd Helen, Menelaus Queene,
With wanton Paris sleepes, and that's the Quarrell.
To Tenedos they come,
And the deepe-drawing Barke do there disgorge
Their warlike frautage: now on Dardan Plaines
The fresh and yet vnbruised Greekes do pitch
Their braue Pauillions. Priams six-gated City,
Dardan and Timbria, Helias, Chetas, Troien,
And Antenonidus with massie Staples
And corresponsiue and fulfilling Bolts
Stirre vp the Sonnes of Troy.
Now Expectation tickling skittish spirits,
On one and other side, Troian and Greeke,
Sets all on hazard. And hither am I come,
A Prologue arm'd, but not in confidence
Of Authors pen, or Actors voyce; but suited
In like conditions, as our Argument;
To tell you (faire Beholders) that our Play
Leapes ore the vaunt and firstlings of those broyles,
Beginning in the middle: starting thence away,
To what may be digested in a Play,
Like, or finde fault, do as your pleasures are,
Now good, or bad, 'tis but the chance of Warre.

THE TRAGEDIE OF
Troylus and Cressida.

Actus Primus. Scœna Prima.

Enter Pandarus and Troylus.

THE THREE ISSUES OF THE FIRST FOLIO

The general outline of the difficulties over *Troilus* had been known before Hinman began his study, but Hinman was the first to realize that there had been two delays: one after the printing of the Catalogue page and another before the Prologue leaf was finally printed. Because Hinman himself overlooked the significance of those delays, it has not usually been realized that during its early days in the bookshops, the Folio was successively sold in three different forms—in other words, that there were three distinct issues of the book.

At least three copies survive in which the only major defect in the body of the book is the complete absence of *Troilus and Cressida*. Many copies, of course, are so defective at the beginning or the end that one or more plays have been lost. Some have major defects elsewhere that include (but are not usually confined to) the loss of a whole play. No other play, however, is so selectively missing as is *Troilus*. One of the copies from which it is absent also lacks the preliminaries, the last two plays, and several single leaves or pairs of leaves from other plays. Another also lacks the preliminaries and the last 11 leaves; the third otherwise lacks only the flyleaf.

During the nineteenth century, many defective Folios were broken up by booksellers in need of odd leaves or quires with which to repair other, less seriously defective copies. The fact that a rebound copy now contains *Troilus* is no guarantee that it always did. Any copy containing only 35 plays would have been considered defective, and a bookseller who acquired one would have been likely either to make it up or break it up. The three copies from which *Troilus and Cressida* is missing probably never contained the play at all, because they were sold before it had been printed.

Three other copies are known which contain the complete *Romeo/Troilus* leaf instead of the Prologue cancel. Another copy with the original leaf now also contains a cancel that is obviously a late insertion taken from a smaller copy. In each copy the redundant page of *Romeo* has been neatly crossed out from corner to corner, and the leaf-signature 'gg3' has been struck through. All four are marked in exactly the same way, and in similar ink. Leaves that were meant to be cancelled and thrown away were not marked in that fashion, but were usually mutilated by cutting or tearing. (In one copy that *has* the Prologue leaf, the torn inner column of the original leaf still survives). There is only one reason why a printer or publisher should take the trouble to have one page crossed out while leaving the other unmarked: to inform the reader that the deleted text should be ignored. The evidence therefore suggests that some copies were sold before the Prologue cancel was printed.

In November 1623, then, the Folio was probably offered for sale before *Troilus and Cressida* was finished. Anyone who bought it obtained a complete book whose contents matched the Catalogue. When *Troilus* was first finished, copies that met the revised definition of 'complete' were assembled and sold before the Prologue was printed. Those who bought one obtained a complete set of 36 plays in which one confusingly redundant page had been helpfully crossed out. Not long afterwards, the remaining copies reached their third and final state of completion when the Prologue was substituted for the crossed-out page.

DEPOSIT AND PRESENTATION COPIES

Two presentation copies of the First Folio survive. Both are copies of the third issue (containing both *Troilus* and its Prologue), probably because Isaac Jaggard waited until he could present copies of Favyn's *Theater of Honour* at the same time. The Favyn preliminaries were not finished until after the rule-frames used in *Troilus* had been dismantled, but the title-page was printed early enough in

Folger copy 1 was presented to Augustine Vincent on behalf of the late William Jaggard in 1623 (probably together with a copy of Favyn's Theater of Honour). *The note recording the gift is in Vincent's handwriting.*

December to be dated 1623 (books finished late in the year were often postdated). It has sometimes been argued that the Favyn title-page must have been printed before William Jaggard died, because he alone is named in the imprint. But in Jaggard's dedication (written when he knew his health was failing), he offers the book to Viscount Mandeville as 'yours by long since precedent promise'. Under the circumstances, Isaac Jaggard's name would have been less appropriate in the imprint than that of his late father.

An agreement of 1611 required London publishers to donate a copy of each new book to Sir Thomas Bodley's library in Oxford. Some publishers ignored the requirement (or complied only on demand, which was often the same thing), but the Jaggards were more conscientious. There is no record of exactly when the copies reached Oxford, but a small batch of books sent to the University's binder on 17 February 1624 included both the Folio and Favyn's *Theater*. The original Bodleian Folio still survives in its 1624 binding. Sold as a duplicate in the 1660s after being replaced by a copy of the Third Folio, it was identified and bought back by the Bodleian Library in 1905.

The other known presentation was a more personal one. Augustine Vincent, whose *Discoverie of Errours* had accompanied the Comedies through the press, was William Jaggard's friend. He was probably involved in some way in the publication of Favyn's *Theater*—he may possibly have been the unidentified translator, but would anyway have been a useful consultant on heraldic questions. If his own copy of Favyn's *Theater* survives, it has not yet been identified. But it is hardly likely that William Jaggard would have wanted to give him the Folio *instead of* Favyn, so he was probably given a copy of each.

Unlike the Bodleian deposit copies, Vincent's copies were probably bound before presentation. His Folio has since been rebound, but the leather of the original front board, impressed with his ar-

morial stamp, is incorporated in the restored binding. On the title-page, Vincent has recorded that the book was given to him by William Jaggard himself. While the gift was undoubtedly made in accordance with William's wishes, it must have been Isaac who actually presented it.

THE FIRST RECORDED PURCHASE

The earliest record of a retail purchase is an entry for 5 December 1623 in the account book of Sir Edward Dering. The 25-year-old Dering, whose interest in the drama during the 1620s and 1630s is amply documented, used to stage plays at his Kent home, Surrenden Hall. Towards the end of 1623 he was in London, and three successive entries in his accounts for 5 December show that in addition to seeing a play (a frequent event), he bought two copies of the Shakespeare Folio and one copy of Ben Jonson's *Workes*.

Unless one of the Folios was intended as a gift, the purchase of two copies suggests that one was for reading and the other for use in his private theatricals. It has been plausibly suggested that a copy now in the University of Padua, in which some of the plays have been annotated for use as prompt copies, may be the Surrenden Hall 'working copy' that Dering bought in December 1623. That copy is also in a binding of the 1620s.

HOW MUCH DID IT COST?

One of the questions most frequently asked about the First Folio is, 'How much did it cost when it was new?' The traditional answer is 'one pound' (20 shillings), but that is only partly true. Three copies are known to have cost a pound each, but another originally cost only 15s. Dering's copy of Jonson's *Workes* cost him 9s.; another copy is known to have cost 10s. A few years later, three

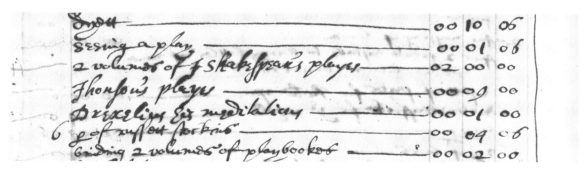

Two entries in Sir Edward Dering's account book show that on 5 December 1623 he bought two copies of the Shakespeare Folio and one copy of Ben Jonson's Workes. *The prices suggest that both Shakespeare Folios were already bound in calf, but that the Jonson volume was probably unbound. The 'J' before Shakespeare's name is not a mistaken initial: Dering apparently began to write the name 'Jhonson' in the wrong entry. (Kent Archives Office: reproduced by permission of the County Archivist.)*

copies of the Second Folio of 1632 were sold for 16s., 18s. 6d., and 22s. respectively. The question of the original price (or prices) therefore deserves a more detailed answer.

Between the compositor and the buyer there were normally three middlemen, each of whom expected to mark up his costs by about 50% to cover his overheads and profit. The printer paid the compositors and pressmen, and charged the publisher half as much again (his mark-up was therefore one-third of what the publisher paid him, and was traditionally known as 'printer's thirds'). The publisher marked up his own costs (which included the paper and the copy) when selling the book at wholesale rates; the bookseller marked up the wholesale price. We can be reasonably certain that a single Folio cost the publishers about 6s. 8d. (about half of which was for the printing, and half for paper and copy), that it was sold wholesale at 10s. to other members of the Stationers' Company, and that an unbound copy would normally have cost 15s. in London.

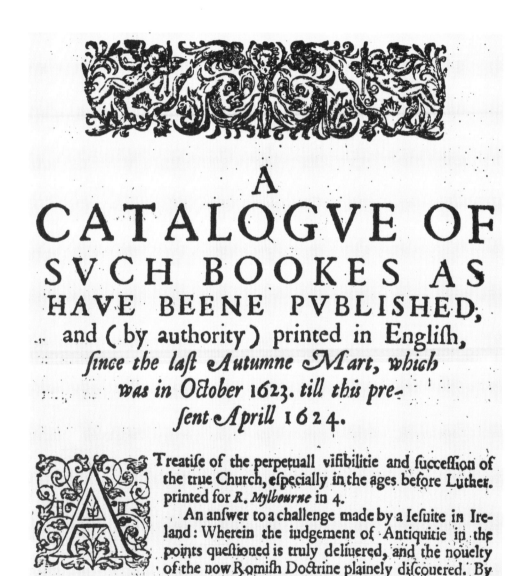

A year and a half after the Jaggards had advertised the forthcoming Folio in the Catalogus Universalis, Edward Blount arranged for the newly completed book to be listed again in the issue for Spring 1624. (Bodleian Library, Oxford: reproduced by permission of the Curators.)

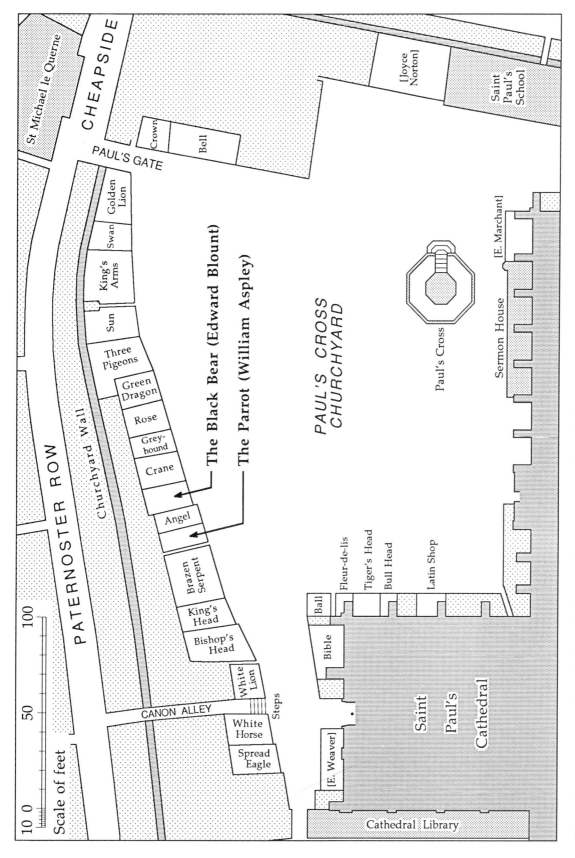

The most important centre of retail bookselling in England was the northeast corner of St Paul's Churchyard. A traditional meeting-place for Londoners since the Middle Ages, the open area was known as Paul's Cross Churchyard (after the open-air pulpit where public sermons were preached every week). All the unshaded properties identified by name or occupant are known to have been bookshops. There were also at least two binderies built against the cathedral to the south of the Latin shop, and some of the shaded properties fronting on the churchyard may also have been occupied by booksellers or binders. Edward Blount's Black Bear was a four-storey building that included both his shop and his dwelling. The ground floor of the neighbouring building was subdivided into two shops, one of which had the sign of the Parrot and was rented by William Aspley.

On the blank flyleaf of Folger copy 71, 'Pretium 15 s' (price 15 shillings) suggests that Thomas Longe bought his copy without a binding. The copy belongs to the second issue (with the crossed-out page of Romeo and Juliet *preceding* Troilus and Cressida*), so the date of purchase was probably November 1623.*

THE WHOLESALE PRICE

A Stationers' Company regulation of 1599 placed an official ceiling on the wholesale prices that could be asked from fellow members of the Company. Production costs varied so widely that for a ceiling to be meaningful at all, it had to allow the publisher to make a reasonable profit, even on a book whose costs had been at the top of the acceptable range. Many books were sold at well below the ceiling price—Jonson's *Workes* cost little more than half what the regulation would have allowed. The limit was introduced only to provide an official definition of excessive overpricing—like a modern speed limit, it was invoked only when conspicuously exceeded. As it applied to books in pica type (the size used in the Folio), the regulation limited the wholesale price to one penny for two sheets unless the book had illustrations. By that rule, the Folio should not have cost more than 9s. 7d., plus a few pence to cover the cost of having the portrait engraved.

The production costs of the Folio must have been near the top of what the acceptable range had been in 1599. The large, two-column pages of pica type took longer to set than did 'average' folio pages (pica was not commonly used in large-paper folios). Using medium quality paper rather than the best available saved no more than about sixpence per copy, and the overall cost of using the playhouse manuscripts and acquiring publication rights would have been high. Furthermore, although the rate of inflation was very low, prices had certainly risen since the 1599 ceiling had been imposed.

The publishers could not risk holding down the price by reducing their mark-up. Doing so would make it necessary to sell a higher percentage of the edition before breaking even—a dangerous gamble, when the market for such a book was virtually untested. (William Aspley and John Smethwick would probably not have joined the principals if the expected profit had been lower

than usual.) But even if the costs had been high enough to justify exceeding the official limit, the risk of overpricing a largely unprecedented book would also have been high.

All the probabilities point to a wholesale price held as close to the 1599 ceiling as costs permitted, or about 10s. per copy. At the customary mark-up, that would mean a retail price of 15s. for an unbound copy. Comparatively few buyers or booksellers wrote purchase prices in books at that date. Those who did so usually wrote them at the top of a flyleaf, and very few surviving Folios have intact flyleaves. One copy, however, still records the original price—a copy of the second issue bought by one Thomas Longe cost him 15s.

THE PUBLISHERS' PROFITS

It has sometimes been claimed that the booksellers named in the imprints or colophons of early books were the exclusive retail agents, but they were not. Most publishers were also retail booksellers, but only a few of the most prolific could have made a living by selling only their own publications.

Of the four publishers of the Folio, three were booksellers by trade (and there was probably a small bookshop on the Barbican frontage of the Jaggard printing house). Each of the publishers would have made about 3s. 4d. from each copy sold wholesale (except on the free copy given to any bookseller who bought 24 copies at once, or who bought a second dozen within six months of buying the first dozen). When they retailed copies from their own shops, however, they added the customary retail mark-up, and thus made 125% over cost.

Copies bought for resale by non-members of the Stationers' Company (usually booksellers from outside London, although there were also London booksellers who belonged to other companies) were customarily discounted at 3s. in the pound of the retail price. Those copies would usually have

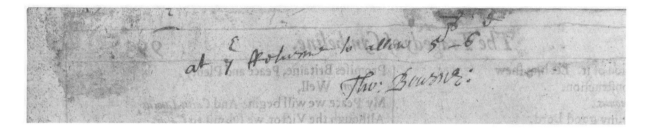

A note on the final blank page of Folger copy 60 apparently indicates that a deposit of 5s. 6d. was to be refunded when this copy was returned to Thomas Bourne (a London bookseller whose independent career began in 1623) by whoever had borrowed it. The circumstances suggest that Bourne 'rented' the book to at least one customer who wished to read it, but not to buy it.

been sold by the publishers themselves at a profit of about 90% over cost (a bookseller who had paid the wholesale price would have made only 22.5% on the same sale). Instead of the Company price of 10s., the price of a Folio to a bookseller outside the Company would have been about 12s. 3d. On top of that, transportation costs would usually have had to be added.

Some provincial booksellers belonged to the Company, and could have sold books at prices similar to those charged in London. Some of them may have used that advantage by underselling their local rivals; others may have made greater profits by matching the usual provincial prices. We can be certain that the retail price was usually higher outside London; it may also have varied more widely.

BORROWING ON DEPOSIT

It is also worth noting that one could read a book without buying it, although disappointingly little is known about the practice. Payments for the loan of books are sometimes recorded in account books (Sir Edward Dering paid for borrowing books of heraldry on several occasions), but the lenders are rarely identifiable as booksellers.

Some booksellers, though, apparently did lend books for a fee. Folger copy 60 has a note on the final blank page: 'at ye Returne to allow 5s–6d'. The note has seemingly been ignored as a casual jotting, but the signature below it is that of a bookseller: Thomas Bourne, freed in January 1623, and working near Bethlehem Hospital in the 1620s and 1630s. The 'Returne' probably refers to the return of the book itself; the sum to be allowed is half the wholesale cost of a Folio, plus half the cost of the cheapest available binding. The most likely interpretation of the note is that Bourne lent out this Folio (perhaps more than once) for an unknown sum that included a 'security deposit' of half the cost of replacing the book.

UNBOUND, READY-BOUND, OR CUSTOM-BOUND

Books were not usually bound before they reached the retailers, and many were not bound until after purchase. (*Most* small books were sold without bindings; the same may have been true of folios, but the percentage was probably lower.) A bookseller who bought several copies at once would have had at least one copy bound in one or other of the 'standard' forms. Most booksellers subcontracted the work to a local bindery, and would have added the price of binding to the cost price before marking up. Some large bookshops had resident binders, and probably increased their profits by matching the usual prices of their rivals. Many purchasers, however, preferred either to commission a specified kind of binding when they paid for the as-yet-unbound book, or else to avoid the bookseller's mark-up by taking the book to a binder themselves.

Most copies would have been bound in one of three styles. Least expensive, though also least common for books larger than quartos, was a limp cover of either vellum (untanned calfskin) or forel (parchment—sheepskin or goatskin—dressed to resemble vellum). Such a cover, which could be had for about a shilling, was thicker and rather more durable than a modern paperback binding, but excessive damp would wrinkle or deform it, and fatigue would eventually crack the hinges.

Forel or vellum could also be used to cover the boards of a hard binding. That would have cost about 2s.—but the skin was still very vulnerable to humidity and fatigue.

The most usual (and most practical) binding for a folio was calf, usually dark brown, on boards of varying thickness and with varying amounts of decoration. If the purchaser of an unbound First Folio took it to an ordinary binder's shop, a plain calf binding would have cost about 3s. or 4s. A London bookseller, however, would probably have marked up the binder's price by his usual 50% when he sold a book ready-bound.

Although no copy of the First Folio is known to have survived in a forel or vellum binding, some copies would undoubtedly have been bound in this fashion either before or after they were first purchased. The cheapest forel bindings were soft covers in which the skin was not reinforced; the book shown above (printed in London in 1614, and bound not long afterwards) has forel-covered boards, which cost about twice as much as a limp binding. Bindings of this kind rarely survive on books that were frequently used. The effects of damp on the skin can be seen at the foot of the front board, while the cracked hinge and the piece broken from the top of the spine show how brittle the skin could become with age.

Most copies of the Folio would originally have been bound in calf, either before sale by the bookseller, or after purchase. Copies bound before sale would not usually have been quite so elaborately decorated as this example (Folger copy 30), which was probably bought without a binding and taken to the purchaser's favourite binder. More than a few copies are still in their original calf bindings, but most are either broken or have been repaired and restored. This copy is unrestored, but the back board is detached and most of the corners are damaged.

The real answer to the question of how much the Folio cost, therefore, is a range rather than a price. In London, unbound copies would usually have cost 15s., while bound copies would have cost about 16s.–17s. in limp forel, 17s.–18s. 6d. in forel-covered boards, and about £1 in plain calf. No copy of the Folio is known to have survived in either kind of forel binding; contemporary calf bindings are not uncommon, but most are either broken or more or less extensively restored.

ABSENT-MINDED BINDERS

Most surviving First Folios have been rebound at least once since the eighteenth century (most commonly in tooled red morocco), but the original binders sometimes left signs of their activity *inside* the book. Among the miscellaneous debris that has often accumulated in the gutter-folds of books in early bindings—wick trimmings, nail parings, pen shavings, grass, crumbs, insects, etc.—it is not at all unusual to find pins that the binder forgot to retrieve. Most are blackened brass pins of various sizes, though one can also find the rusted remains of iron or steel pins and (much more rarely) large needles.

Traces of even larger objects are sometimes found, especially metal objects left in books long enough to corrode or rust. One Folger Folio contains the rusted outline of a pair of spectacles; another, what appears to have been a large key. Other books in the collection have been similarly marked by coins, a table knife, etc. Most of those were probably left in the books by readers.

It would be exaggerating to call such traces 'common' at all, but among the objects of which outlines have been found in books of this period, one particular implement has left its mark sufficiently often to require special explanation. A number of books have been found to contain the rusted outlines of pairs of scissors, mostly of very similar size and design. Since scissors are rarely used as either reading aids or as bookmarks, the most likely explanation is that binders sometimes left them in books by accident. By some statistical freak, the Folger collection includes no fewer than *three* Folios in which pairs of scissors were once left, probably by the original binders.

EARLY PURCHASERS AND OWNERS

Luckily for the publishers, the First Folio was a commercial success, and when it sold out there was still enough of a demand to justify a second edition in 1632. It broke no records, but selling out

inside nine years was a respectable performance for a fairly expensive folio.

We have, unfortunately, almost no reliable information about who bought First Folios during those first nine years. Relatively few seventeenth-century owners inscribed their books, and fewer still used bookplates or personal binding stamps. Those who did so (and who were probably not 'typical' owners) usually recorded their ownership on the most vulnerable parts of the book, which in most cases have now disappeared.

To the original purchasers, and to most people who bought second-hand copies before the mid-1700s, the Folio was not a historical artifact to preserve for future study, but a book to read and use. With repeated use, bindings cracked and boards became detached. Flyleaves were torn out to be used as blank paper; careless handling crumpled and tore the leaves at both ends of the book. When a board broke off, some of the leaves next to it often broke away too, and were eventually discarded or lost.

Meanwhile, the plays were reprinted in 1632, 1663, and 1685, edited in 1709, and then reprinted and reedited with increasing frequency. To most owners before the late eighteenth century, a First Folio was merely an outdated book in poor condition. When its unique importance began to be more widely recognized, collectors who obtained copies usually had them cleaned, rebound, and (if necessary) perfected with leaves from copies in worse condition. That process often destroyed all evidence of earlier ownership.

THEATRICAL OWNERS AND USERS

Whether or not most playgoers were also interested in buying plays to read (which is uncertain), it is safe to assume that most purchasers of the Folio were at least occasional playgoers. The book would also presumably have interested some playwrights and would-be playwrights, professional and amateur actors, and patrons of private theatricals such as Sir Edward Dering. But with the exception of the copy now in Padua that may have been Dering's, no surviving copy has been credibly connected with any playwright, actor, or performance before the Restoration. If such copies existed, they may have been annotated, and may eventually have been discarded precisely because they *were* annotated. But for whatever reason, no copy ever owned or used by any of Shakespeare's colleagues, rivals, or immediate successors in the theatre is known to survive.

When the Third Folio was published in 1663, it was a simple reprint of the Second, and contained

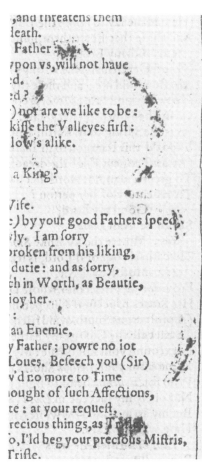

,and threatens them
death.
Father
pon vs, will not haue
d.
d?
) not are we like to be :
kiffe the Valleyes firft :
low's alike.

a King?

ife.
) by your good Fathers fpeed,
ly. I am forry
roken from his liking,
dutie : and as forry,
ch in Worth, as Beautie,
ioy her.

an Enemie,
y Father ; powre no iot
Loues. Befeech you (Sir)
v'd no more to Time
ought of fuch Affections,
te : at your requeft,
recious things, as T
o, I'ld beg your precious Miftris,
Trifle.

Metal objects left in books by readers sometimes remained in place long enough to corrode or rust, as did the spectacles that were once left in Folger copy 46 (Comedies, page 300), shown at the left.

Scissors, however, are not used as reading aids sufficiently often to account for the frequency with which their outlines are found in early books. The person most likely to leave a pair of scissors in a book was the original binder.

The impression shown at the right is found in Folger copy 63 (Tragedies, page 298). That copy is assembled from fragments of others, and the adjacent leaf is from a different original copy. The mirror image of the same scissors may survive on page 299 of another made-up Folio.

Shown below are two other examples, found in Folger copy 58 (Histories, pages 50–1, at left) and Folger copy 67 (Comedies, pages 48–9, at right).

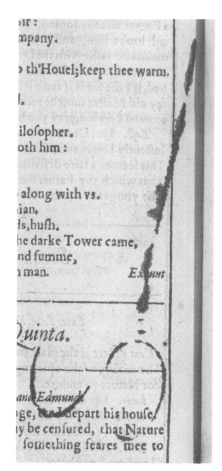

r :
mpany.

o th'Houel ; keep thee warm.

ilofopher.
oth him :

along with vs.
ian,
s, hufh.
he darke Tower came,
nd fumme,
man.   Exeunt

Quinta.

Edmund
ge,   depart his houfe,
y be cenfured, that Nature
fomething feares mee to

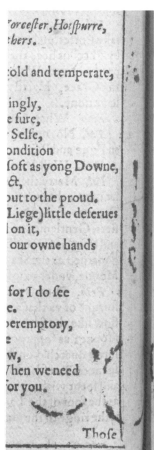

orcefter, Hotfpurre,
hers.

old and temperate,

ingly,
e fure,
Selfe,
ondition
foft as yong Downe,
ct,
ut to the proud.
Liege) little deferues
on it,
our owne bands

for I do fee
e.
eremptory,

w,
hen we need
or you.

Thofe

Which many a good I an
So Cowardly. And but for
He would himfelfe haue be
This bald, vnioynted Chat
Made me to anfwer indire
And I befeech you, let not
Come currant for an Accuf
Betwixt my Loue, and your
Blunt. The circumftance
What euer Harry Percie th
To fuch a perfon, and in fu
At fuch a time, with all the
May reafonably dye, and he
To do him wrong, or any w
What then he faid, fo he vi
King. Why yet doth de
But with poui?o and Exce
That we at our owne charg
His Brother-in-Law, the fe
Who (in my foule) hath wi
The liues of thofe, that he
Againft the great Magitiat
Whofe daughter (as we he
Hath lately married. Shal
Be emptied, to redeeme a
Shall we buy Treafon? and
When they haue loft and fe

ted withall.
e man fhould fight with

weapons : keepe them a-
m.
keepe in your weapon,
Doctor.
them queftion : let them
k our Englifh.
peake a word with your
t-a me?
ence in good time.
ard : de Iack dog : Iohn

aughing-ftocks to other
iendfhip, and I will one
I will knog your Vrinal
e.
ne Hoft de Iarteer : haue I
ue I not at de place I did

foule, now looke you :
bee iudgement by mine

d Gaule, French & Welch,

Cai. I,

Ford. Well met miftris
M.Pa. Truly Sir, to fee
Ford. I, and as idle as f
of company : I thinke if y
two would marry.
M.Pa. Be fure of that,
Ford. Where had you
M.Pa. I cannot tell wh
husband had him of, what
Rob. Sir Iohn Falftaffe.
Ford. Sir Iohn Falftaffe.
M.Pa. He, I can neue
league betweene my goo
Ford. Indeed fhe is.
M.Pa. By your leaue fi
Ford. Has Page any brai
any thinking? Sure they
why this boy will carrie
a Canon will fhoot point
ces out his wiues inclinat
and aduantage : and now
ftaffes boy with her : A m
in the winde ; and Falftaf
they are laide, and our re
together : Well, I will ta
plucke the borrowed vail
ming Mift. Page, divulge

only the 36 plays found in the First. In the following year it was reissued with seven additional plays inserted as if Shakespeare's (the only one now accepted is *Pericles*). The publication of that book materially affected the survival of the First Folio, because copies of the new edition were not only in better condition, but also 'more complete'. The Bodleian Library was undoubtedly not alone in deciding that the Third Folio superseded the First, and private owners may likewise have sold 'old' Folios when buying new ones. By the 1670s, First Folios could probably be acquired very cheaply as second-hand books. It may therefore be no coincidence that while no surviving copy can be linked with the professional theatre before the Restoration, at least three copies have theatrical pedigrees beginning in the 1660s or 1670s.

The earliest English playwright known to have owned a First Folio is William Congreve (1670–1729), whose copy had formerly belonged to Charles Killigrew. Killigrew himself became Master of the Revels and a patentee of the Drury Lane Theatre in 1677. It has been suggested that the Congreve copy may once have belonged to Charles's playwright father, Thomas Killigrew the elder. There is, however, no evidence for that, and Killigrew senior could hardly have been the *first* owner. The Congreve copy is one of those that contains neither *Troilus and Cressida* nor any evidence of its former presence. It is probably a copy of the first issue, sold in early November 1623 when Thomas Killigrew was only 11 years old.

Folger copy 73, which belonged to someone with theatrical interests in or before the 1670s, has also been wrongly supposed to have belonged to Thomas Killigrew. In addition to compiling lists of *dramatis personæ* beside two comedies, the owner drew attention to a few comic scenes that he particularly enjoyed, and commented that *The Taming of the Shrew* might be made into 'somthing prety… in Pastarole'. Near the foot of one page of *The Winter's Tale*, the same hand has unobtrusively inserted the abbreviated name, 'T: Killig'. But the handwriting is not Killigrew's, and another playwright's name is similarly noted in the margin of a page of *Antony and Cleopatra*: Sir Charles Sedley (abbreviated as 'sr chãr sid:') wrote his own play of *Antony and Cleopatra* in 1677. Ten years earlier, Killigrew's company had performed an adaptation of *The Taming of the Shrew* (called *Sauny the Scot*) by the comedian John Lacy. Whether or not that was quite the 'Pastarole' he had in mind, the owner of Folger copy 73 was certainly interested in, and familiar with, the professional theatre of his day.

The copy with the most obvious theatrical provenance has unfortunately survived only in a few fragments—perhaps discarded because it was a heavily annotated working copy. Edinburgh University Library has two separately bound plays taken from a defective copy in which at least some of the plays were marked for use as prompt copies. *A Midsummer Night's Dream* (with four leaves from a different copy) has been heavily cut, but it lacks the characteristic signs of actual use during a performance. Such signs are, however, found in *A Comedy of Errors* (with the final leaf from a different copy), and the actors named in the 'calls' for entrance suggest that the play was performed around 1672 at the Hatton Garden theatre known as the Nursery.

While materials were being selected for this exhibition, six leaves of a third 'Nursery promptbook' were discovered among the uncatalogued Folger collection of fragments. Four of the leaves were found in a made-up copy of *Macbeth*, *Hamlet*, and *King Lear*. Another leaf was found in a second made-up copy of the same plays, and the sixth in a miscellaneous collection of single leaves. It therefore seems likely that fragments of the 'Nursery' Folio were used by at least one nineteenth-century bookseller for making up other copies, and that more leaves may yet be discovered.

THE FIRST FOLIO BECOMES OBSOLETE

The Fourth Folio of 1685 was the last Folio to be simply reprinted from its predecessor (the Third, with the seven additional plays), and by the early 1700s the plays were coming to be seen as works that required editing. In the Fourth Folio, as in the Second and the Third, many obvious misprints found in the previous edition had been corrected, and the spelling, punctuation, and sometimes even the language, had been 'modernized'. Inevitably, each reprint introduced new errors of its own, 'corrected' readings that had not in fact been errors, and made wrong guesses when emending genuine mistakes.

The earliest editors failed to realize that the later Folios were all textually inferior to the First. Nicholas Rowe used the Fourth Folio as the basis of his 1709 edition, and while he made many genuine and perceptive corrections, he also accepted (or mistakenly corrected) readings that had originated as misprints in one or other of the later Folios. While two of the next four editors did at least *examine* the First Folio, and restored some of its readings, each of them based his edition on the preceding one—with the usual consequences.

A 'typical' owner of a First Folio would have been largely unaware of the editors' failings. Not only was the book an aged copy containing fewer

Folger copy 73 contains several annotations made by a Restoration owner, including the note shown above at the end of The Taming of the Shrew *(Comedies, page 229). The comment suggests that 'somthing prety might be made of this in Pastarole' (i.e. pastoral).*

On the strength of the abbreviated name written in the text of The Winter's Tale *(Comedies, page 295), it has been suggested that the annotator of copy 73 was the playwright Thomas Killigrew the elder (1612–85). Neither the supposed signature nor the annotations, however, are in Killigrew's handwriting.*

The two pages shown below are from a copy of Hamlet *that was annotated for use (but never actually used) as a prompt copy. Two nearly complete plays from the same original Folio, annotated in the same fashion, are in Edinburgh University Library, and are known as the 'Nursery prompt-books' because they are believed to have been marked for use in the Nursery theatre in Hatton Garden, London, in the 1670s. The two leaves illustrated, and four others (also from* Hamlet*), were recently discovered among the uncatalogued fragments in the Folger collection.*

plays than its successors, but the plays as printed in 1623 were evidently corrupt. Why else should editor after editor find it necessary to improve on the combined efforts of his predecessors? It seems likely that more First Folios would have been discarded between 1700 and 1750 than in any other half-century.

THE REVIVAL OF INTEREST

By the middle of the eighteenth century, however, editors had begun to realize that the First Folio was far more important than its successors. Two major editions appeared in the 1760s, each with a preface in which the editor pointed out that the later Folios were merely inferior reprints of the First. Dr Johnson expressed it most influentially in his edition of 1765, although his editorial use of the Folios fell far short of his stated principle. Edward Capell, who had spent two decades actually practising what Johnson eventually preached, wrote such tortuous prose that when his edition finally appeared in 1768, the preface received far less attention than it deserved.

But while Johnson and Capell were among the first to say so in print, others had already begun to recognize that the First Folio was indispensable to the serious study of Shakespeare. And since arguing about Shakespeare's text had become something of a national pastime since the 1720s, the growing recognition of the First Folio's unique importance soon evolved into a growing demand for copies.

BREAKING UP AND MAKING UP

By the late 1770s that demand was so great that the practice of breaking up one defective Folio to complete another had become common. What the literary scholar or enthusiast wanted most was a *complete* copy—not so much because copies in mint condition were more highly prized as collectors' items (although there were certainly some collectors in search of 'perfect' copies), but because in the absence of photographic facsimiles, only a complete copy contained the complete 1623 text. To potential editors and commentators, completeness mattered more than condition, because their need was for working copies (which many of them would then proceed to annotate). By 1778 one bookseller had apparently managed to sell two leaves from a broken copy for two guineas (£2 2s.), which the outraged George Steevens claimed was a quarter of what had recently been the usual price of a complete copy. Fifteen years

later, Steevens had become equally disturbed by the increased frequency of sophistication: the use of leaves from Second Folios, and of specially printed facsimile title-pages, to make defective copies seem more complete.

The motive for sophisticating an imperfect copy was usually honest: to create an *appearance* of completeness, but not necessarily an illusion. Unscrupulous booksellers certainly existed, and it can hardly be doubted that some sophisticated copies were deliberately passed off as perfect. Unless the new owner compared his copy with a perfect one, or eventually learned how to distinguish a real leaf from an imitation, an imposture could remain undetected for decades. More often, though, the sophistication was unconcealed—sometimes, indeed, it may have been commissioned at the time of purchase, or arranged at a later date, as a service analogous to binding. Such copies were more likely to be misrepresented when they were *next* sold, because there were probably as many ignorant booksellers as dishonest ones.

The leaves that most frequently needed to be repaired or replaced were the preliminaries (especially the flyleaf and title) and the last few leaves of *Cymbeline*. Replacements were less commonly needed at the back of the book than at the front, but were more essential to the text. For someone with no plans to study the text minutely, Second Folio leaves were the easiest solution, perhaps with the colophon date either erased or altered to 1623. Anyone planning a close study would have preferred a careful pen facsimile, copied or traced from a perfect example. Some nineteenth-century facsimilists, including the legendary John Harris, could produce copies so convincing that even an expert eye can occasionally miss them.

In a scholar's working copy, the preliminaries mattered less than the plays themselves. The absence of one or more preliminary leaves had little effect on the textual value of the book, and could sometimes be tolerated. Otherwise, Second Folio leaves were acceptable to many. The one exception was the leaf which every owner wanted, and without which even a battered working copy seemed unacceptably defective, namely the title leaf.

THE QUEST FOR TITLE-PAGES

So long as a replacement title-page bore a general resemblance to the original, it seems that few owners before the 1860s demanded the same kind of accuracy they expected in the plays themselves. Some copies have hand-drawn title-pages, not copied closely enough to qualify as pen facsimiles. Others have the kind of printed facsimiles about

PREFACE.

In his reports of copies and editions he is not to be trufted, without examination. He fpeaks fometimes indefinitely of copies, when he has only one. In his enumeration of editions, he mentions the two firft folios as of high, and the third folio as of middle authority; but the truth is, that the firft is equivalent to all others, and that the reft only deviate from it by the printer's negligence. Whoever has any of the folios has all, excepting thofe diverfities which mere reiteration of editions will produce. I collated them all at the beginning, but afterwards ufed only the firft.

Some of our legitimate editions will afford a fufficient fpecimen of the fluctuation of price in books.—An ancient quarto was fold for fix pence; and the folios 1623 and 1632, when firft printed, could not have been rated higher than at ten fhillings each.—Very lately, one, and two guineas, have been paid for a quarto; the firft folio is ufually valued at feven or eight: but what price may be expected for it hereafter, is not very eafy to be determined, the confcience of Mr. Fox, bookfeller in Holborn, having lately permitted him to afk no lefs than *two guineas* for *two leaves* out of a mutilated copy of that impreffion, though he had feveral, almoft equally defective, in his fhop. The fecond folio is commonly rated at two or three guineas.

[6] Every poffible adulteration has of late years been practifed in fitting up copies of this book for fale.

When leaves have been wanting, they have been reprinted with battered types, and foifted into vacancies, without notice of fuch defects and the remedies applied to them.

When the title has been loft, a fpurious one has been fabricated, with a blank fpace left for the head of Shakfpeare, afterwards added from the fecond, third, or fourth impreffion. To conceal thefe frauds, thick vermillion lines have been ufually drawn over the edges of the engravings, which would otherwife have betrayed themfelves when let into a fupplemental page, however craftily it was lined at the back, and difcoloured with tobacco-water till it had affumed the true *jaune antique*.

Sometimes leaves have been inferted from the fecond folio, and, in a known inftance, the entire play of *Cymbeline*; the genuine date at the end of it [1632] having been altered into 1623.

which Steevens complained: printed copies of the lines of letterpress, with a blank space for the portrait. There are at least three varieties, one of them presumably the version mentioned by Steevens in 1793. Another, probably later, is easily identified by the misprint 'WILIAM' in the first line.

If the portrait in a damaged title-page was sufficiently intact, pasting it on to the facsimile was essentially an act of repair rather than replacement. Original title-pages were obviously in short supply, so it is unlikely that many were sold to be used in that way. If the portrait pasted on one of those facsimile leaves can be shown to come from a First Folio, it is more likely than not to be the remains of the original title-page. More commonly, however, a portrait was taken from one of the later Folios—usually the Second, in which the engraving is indistinguishable from the third state of 1623 (although the edition can be identified by the paper if the watermark is visible). In some copies with title-pages of this kind, the portrait is from a later Folio; in others it is simply drawn in by hand. A few copies have no portrait at all—but it is uncertain whether they reflect bibliographical integrity, lack of opportunity, or the failure to use a permanent adhesive.

The first 'type-facsimile' edition (a line-for-line, letter-for-letter reprint) was published in 1807, with a portrait printed from a newly engraved copy of the original engraving. For the next half-century, that title-page became the usual substitute for the real thing, and may sometimes have been used to replace earlier improvisations. Extra copies may have been printed for that very purpose, most of them on the paper made especially for the edition (watermarked 'SHAKESPEARE 1806'). It would appear that shortly after the 1807 title-page had been printed, the lines of type were reimposed (the spacing of the lines is not quite the same) and used with the engraving to print a few title-pages on seventeenth-century paper. Those copies, which do not identify the printer on the reverse, may have been intended to deceive.

The first photolithographic facsimile of the Folio was printed in 1866, and it soon became the most common source not only for title-pages, but for all replacement leaves. Fragments of the facsimile were also used to patch defective original leaves, and at least one owner used pieces cut out of the 1866 title to convert a Second Folio title-page (perhaps already bound into his copy) into something more closely resembling a First.

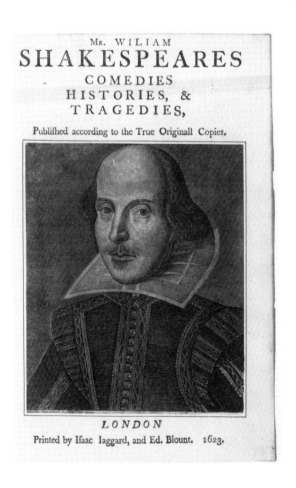

Shown below are four examples of the many kinds of faked and facsimile title-pages now found in First Folios.

At the extreme left, Folger copy 42 still has much of the original title-page. The amateur repairs illustrate how little trouble was sometimes taken to reproduce the original appearance with any fidelity.

The second illustration on the facing page shows a reprint of the lines of text, with the portrait from a Second Folio pasted in the space provided (Folger copy 41). There are at least three reprints of this kind, one of them mentioned by George Steevens in 1793. The version shown is probably later. Had Steevens seen the misprinted 'WILIAM' in the first line, he would almost certainly have mentioned it.

The title-page below is from a type-facsimile edition published in 1807. The re-engraved portrait shows a somewhat nobler, more respectable playwright than does the original engraving. This title-page (illustrated from Folger copy 52) was often used before the 1860s to supply the place of a lost or damaged original, and is found in several Folger copies.

Illustrated at the right is a Second Folio title-page. Below it is another copy, bound into a First Folio (Folger copy 78) and patched with pieces taken from the 1866 facsimile in a partly successful attempt to make it look more authentic.

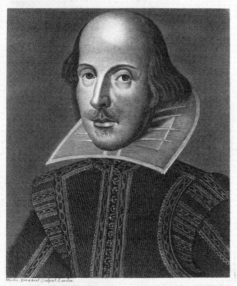

When possible, the owners of imperfect Folios preferred to have missing leaves supplied from other original copies. More seriously defective copies were therefore used by booksellers as sources of replacement leaves. During the nineteenth century, booksellers began to trade the shrinking remnants of such copies among themselves. Some of the copies whose remains entered that circulating collection of 'scrap' Folios were quite recognizable. A few were annotated in idiosyncratic fashion; others were distinctively re-margined, had been cut to unusual dimensions, or showed other distinguishing features such as coloured edges, localized worm-damage, etc. Leaves from those copies can often be identified in the made-up Folios in which they now survive. One of the easiest to identify is a copy once owned by a scholar who apparently planned to edit the plays, and who annotated his First Folio when comparing it line by line with the later Folios and the major editions before 1750. Leaves from that annotated copy have been found in three of the Folger copies, and there are others among the uncatalogued fragments.

By the end of the nineteenth century, the First Folio was becoming noticeably more difficult to acquire. While the book was far from rare, many of the best copies had been acquired by institutional libraries. Meanwhile, American collectors were increasingly able and eager to outbid their English rivals, and so more and more copies were emigrating. Booksellers therefore began to look anew at copies they had previously cannibalized for the sake of others, and the best of those copies in turn were made up from the dwindling supply of copies in even worse condition. Soon, both booksellers and collectors were attempting to assemble new 'copies' from miscellaneous collections of single leaves in every imaginable condition. Now it was the turn of individual leaves to supply each others' defects, and damaged leaves were sometimes patched with pieces cut from more seriously defective ones.

It is usually estimated that about 230 or 240 copies of the First Folio survive. But that figure includes 'copies' made up from fragments—in some cases, fragments from more than a dozen broken copies. The number of original copies of which *parts* survive is probably closer to 300.

Folger copy 63 is a made-up copy assembled from parts of several broken copies. The leaf shown at the right (Tragedies, page 59) is one of five taken from a copy annotated by a scholar who may have planned to edit the plays. The notes record the results of comparing the First Folio with each of the three later Folios and the five major eighteenth-century editions before 1750.

A reduced facsimile of the First Folio was published in 1876. Shortly after his marriage in 1885, Henry Clay Folger gave a copy to his wife, so that she could 'see Shakespeare's plays as they were actually given to the world'. Four years later he bought his first early edition of the plays: a copy of the Fourth Folio. Thus began the formation of the largest and most important collection of printed Shakespeare that has ever been assembled.

Folger's first Shakespeare purchase had been an edition he bought during his senior year at Amherst, after Emerson's 'Remarks at the Celebration of the Three Hundredth Anniversary of the Birth of Shakespeare' had persuaded him to study the plays. After graduating in 1879, he took a job as a clerk with Charles Pratt and Company, part of the Standard group of oil refineries. He also began to study law at Columbia, receiving his LL.B. *cum laude* and being admitted to the New York Bar in 1881. Four years later he married Emily Clara Jordan, who had been educated at Vassar.

Before their marriage, neither of the Folgers could have been called a serious student of Shakespeare, but their shared enthusiasm soon became the main focus of their lives. As Henry rose through the ranks at the Standard Oil Company (becoming president in 1911, and chairman of the board in 1923), he used his increasing wealth to expand his growing collection of books. Meanwhile he and Emily were making themselves familiar with all the major scholarly works on Shakespeare, and Emily eventually submitted a thesis for an M.A. degree in English literature, which she received from Vassar in 1896.

From the beginning, the main focus of Henry Folger's collecting was on the Folio editions of Shakespeare, especially the First. That is not to say that he ignored the Quartos or the poems—his collection of those books alone has few rivals, and his acquisition of the unique 1594 Quarto of *Titus Andronicus* was one of the greatest triumphs of his career—and he accumulated a huge collection of Shakespeareana of all kinds. But he rarely allowed his pursuit of Shakespearean source-material, works of scholarship, theatrical relics, playbills, portraits, and other Shakespeare memorabilia to distract him from an opportunity to acquire yet another choice Folio.

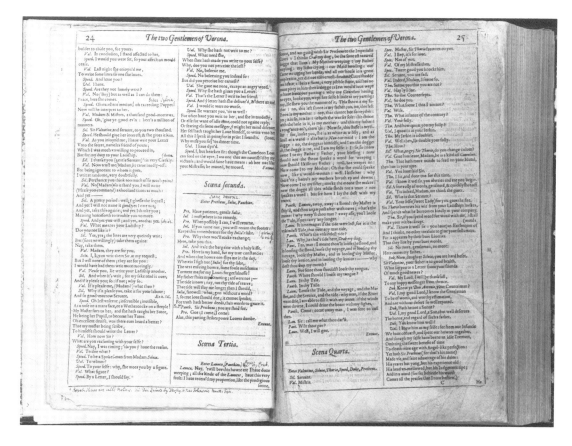

Folger copy 76, once owned by Thomas Percy, Bishop of Dromore, at one time lacked the preliminaries and the first 12 leaves of text. Those leaves were later supplied from another copy, and the illustration above shows the last page of the added section (Comedies, page 24). The copy from which the 12 leaves were taken was the same annotated copy that supplied five leaves to copy 63, shown on the facing page.

Henry Clay Folger

Emily Jordan Folger

In 1928, Folger formally announced that he intended to build a library in Washington, to house his collection as a gift to the nation. Two weeks after the foundation stone was laid in 1930, he died of a heart attack, and never saw the final realization of his dream. But by the time he died, he had managed to collect more copies of each of the Folios than had ever been assembled in one place since each was first published—including approximately one-third of the surviving copies of the First Folio itself.

Like all endeavours of mythic proportion, Henry Folger's collecting has generated many myths. It is sometimes claimed that until the books were unpacked, not even the Folgers realized exactly how many First Folios Henry had acquired. In fact, they kept careful records of his purchases, and while not courting publicity, made no secret of the size of the collection. When Henry acquired his fortieth copy, their friend H. H. Furness (the distinguished Shakespearean scholar and editor) dubbed him 'Forty Folio Folger'. When the total reached 49, Folger was delighted to take ex-President Taft's hint that 'We have the fiftieth at Yale', and to complete the half-century by acquiring a copy from the Elizabethan Club. Nor is it true that Folger's plan to build a research library was a secret known only to Emily before he announced it in 1928. In a talk (later printed) that she gave in November 1923, Emily openly commented that

'With the thought of a Shakespeare Library which may serve the students to come, Mr. Folger has rather specialized in First Folios.'

Other myths have surrounded Emily and her M.A. thesis. On the one hand, it is sometimes claimed that while Henry had the money, the brains belonged to Emily; that she was ahead of her time in recognizing the textual importance of comparing copies in search of variants. On the other hand, she is sometimes accused of believing that only by comparing copies could one at last reveal 'The True Text of Shakespeare' (the title of her thesis). Neither suggestion is true. Emily's thesis is an unexceptional example of its genre and date, and follows the then-prevailing rules by arguing, point by point, to an unexceptional conclusion. Every point is made by quoting or citing an accepted authority, and the pros and cons are argued by quoting or citing others. There are no obvious signs of originality (especially on textual questions)—but neither is there any evidence of eccentricity.

It appears to be true that the motive behind Henry's almost obsessive desire to acquire as many First Folios as possible was the belief that it was important to collate large numbers of copies so that all the variants could be found. Whether it was Henry or Emily who first learned that such variants existed is uncertain—but the fact had been known to scholars since at least the 1840s.

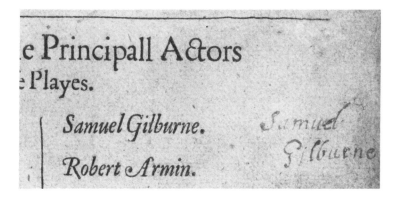

Shown at top left is the supposed signature of Samuel Gilburne in Folger copy 12. Also shown are two examples of the same kind of annotation. In Folger copy 58, the name of John Rice has been copied below the list of actors, possibly by a child, and in copy 70 the first two lines of Ben Jonson's commendatory verse have been copied beside the printed text. Annotation of this kind is so common that the Gilburne 'signature' is far more likely to be yet another example than to be the actor's autograph. It is not known whether Gilburne was still alive in 1623, and no verifiable example of his handwriting has been found.

It is also true that the Folgers believed that a study of the variants would help to establish 'The True Text'—but only in the reasonable sense that it would establish the text of the Folio itself. The title of Emily's thesis alludes specifically to the First Folio, of which she concluded that 'If it is not Shakespeare's text, it is, as Furness says, the nearest possible approach to it.'

THE PURSUIT OF THE 'GILBURNE' COPY

When Folger began to buy First Folios, he bought whatever copies were available, and some years passed before he acquired his first complete copy. During the middle years of his collecting career he was able to be more discriminating, and he turned down several copies that he considered inferior or overpriced. But when he set his sights on a particular copy, he could pursue it doggedly.

One such copy was described in a London catalogue in May 1919 as being 'probably' the copy originally owned by Samuel Gilburne, one of the 'Principall Actors' listed in the Folio preliminaries. Almost nothing is known about Gilburne except that he had served his apprenticeship with the actor Augustine Phillips before 1605, and was mentioned in Phillips's will. Next to the printed name in that copy, Gilburne's name was written, or perhaps signed, in an early hand.

The Folio was imperfect and not unreasonably priced, so Folger ordered it. But it had already been bought by Gabriel Wells of New York on behalf of an unidentified client who had apparently seen an advance copy of the catalogue. Folger wrote to Wells in June, asking him to find out if the owner would sell the Folio back, if necessary at a higher price. He wrote again in August and October, but was eventually told that the owner had shown little interest. In November he offered $6,000—nearly double the original catalogue price—but the owner still wanted a First Folio, and was unwilling to sell the only one he had.

In January 1920 Wells offered Folger a fine copy at $11,500. Instead of buying it, Folger suggested a deal: it should be offered to the owner of the Gilburne copy at a price consisting of the Gilburne copy itself plus $3,000, and if the offer was accepted, Folger would pay the difference. The $3,000, however, was apparently more than the owner was willing to pay. Three months later, in March, Wells offered Folger another good copy. Folger proposed a similar exchange with a balance of only $2,300, but was again turned down. Some of the later correspondence is missing, but Folger finally acquired the Gilburne copy in May 1920. He appears to have simply exchanged it for a copy he had bought at auction for $8,800.

Regrettably, there is no more than a very remote possibility that the so-called Gilburne copy ever belonged to the actor, and Folger must have known that the attribution rested on the flimsiest of evidence. The name does not look very like a signature, and copying a name, word, or phrase beside the printed original is a very common form of early 'doodling'. But no specimen of Gilburne's hand is known, so it is impossible to be certain that the copy was *not* his, and Folger was willing and eager to take the chance, just in case.

THE VINCENT SAGA

Folger's collection of First Folios includes several fine copies, two of them among the finest in existence, but the copy he prized most of all is not even complete. That copy, placed at the head of the list when he assigned numbers to his first 66 copies, is the Folio presented to Augustine Vincent in 1623 on behalf of William Jaggard.

The Vincent copy was discovered in 1891 by the bookseller A. B. Railton, in the collection of Coningsby Sibthorp at Canwick Hall, Lincolnshire. Imperfect, in a broken binding tied with string, neglected in a dusty stack of folios on top of a bookcase in the coach house, it was thrown down to Railton by a helper who commented, 'That is no good, sir, it is only old poetry.'

Realizing its value, Railton had the volume restored for Sibthorp, supplying all but two of the missing leaves from another copy, and the flyleaf and final leaf in facsimile. It was carefully rebound in imitation of the original binding, without trimming, and with the stamped leather from the original front board incorporated. The question of trimming was important, because while it is not quite true that the Vincent copy is wholly uncut (the first binder seems to have trimmed it enough to remove the most extreme irregularities from the deckle edge of the largest leaves), no known copy is closer to that ideal. When Railton returned it to Sibthorp, he hinted that he would be interested in purchasing it, but met with a polite refusal.

While in Railton's hands, the copy was inspected by experts at the British Museum, and Sidney Lee later described it in an article. Folger learned of its existence through that article, and later saw a copy of the Museum report. In March 1899 he asked Railton to approach Sibthorp on his behalf. Railton proceeded cautiously, but in June he reported partial success. Sibthorp had named the unprecedented price of £5,000 (well over $20,000), believing and perhaps hoping that it would be prohibitive. Folger offered £4,000, half in cash and half on 1 January 1900, but Sibthorp repeated that his price was £5,000. Folger asked Railton to try again with £4,500. He could settle for £5,000 if necessary, but only £2,000 could be paid before January 1.

Knowing that Sibthorp would retract his offer unless it was accepted unconditionally, Railton obeyed only in part: he used his discretion and offered £5,000, which Sibthorp accepted. He was not pleased to find out later that Folger wanted terms. January 1 was acceptable, and Folger could pay Railton as and when he chose, but Sibthorp expected a simple exchange—the book for £5,000. By November he was perhaps regretting that he had named a price at all. In Folger's view the sale had been secured when he sent Railton the first £2,000, and he wanted the book put in safe storage until January. In Sibthorp's view no sale had yet taken place, and he resented the suggestion that his book might not be safe at Canwick Hall.

In December, disaster struck. Folger had read Lee's article and the Museum report, so Railton had assumed that he was fully aware of the condition of the book—but neither source had given a full description. Another bookseller now described it to him rather disparagingly, and Folger learned for the first time that he was about to pay a record-breaking price for a copy that had two leaves in facsimile. When he demanded an explanation, Railton assured him that he had never been intentionally misled, but Folger still felt aggrieved. He had offered £5,000 in the belief that all the leaves were genuine: he would pay that price if the facsimile leaves were replaced, but otherwise would pay only £4,000. Railton warned him that trying to revise the terms could be fatal, so Folger sent the remaining £3,000 on the 19th. But on the 22nd he imposed new conditions: no money was to change hands until Folger had received and inspected the book. Caught between two determined men, Railton did what he could, but he could not complete the sale on time without Folger's permission. On January 3, Sibthorp instructed him to return the original £2,000, because he no longer wished to sell. Folger's response was 'Buy without condition' (though even then he asked Railton to secure, if possible, the right to sell the book back at £4,800 after inspection).

But Sibthorp was no longer willing. On the 6th he declined the renewed offer; on the 7th Folger offered £6,000 without condition. He was at last beginning to see that Sibthorp's refusal to bargain had not been an attempt to hold him to an unfair price that he had accepted in ignorance. Sibthorp genuinely treasured the book. Naming a prohibitive price had been his way of saying 'take it or leave it', and Folger had done neither. Haggling was not Sibthorp's way: naming one price while being prepared to accept another was less than gentlemanly. The ever-changing strings that had been attached to the money had irritated him; he preferred to own a book that he could cherish in peace and quiet.

During January, Folger seemed almost frantic. For the first time he wrote directly to Sibthorp, to explain how and why he had reacted so strongly in December. Meanwhile, he told Railton that for £6,000 Sibthorp could, if he wished, keep the book in his possession for up to five years after selling it. On the 15th he cabled Railton twice: first to offer up to £8,000; then to ask whether it might help if he came to London in person. The next day he cabled again, in case Railton had not realized that even the new offer would allow Sibthorp to keep the book for up to five years. Railton had already mentioned the offer of £6,000, but he knew that if pressured, Sibthorp might declare the subject permanently closed. He advised Folger that the only safe course was to wait patiently.

In the summer of 1902, Railton hesitantly informed Sibthorp that Folger was still interested. Without asking for details, Sibthorp reassured him that the subject was not forbidden—he could mention it, say, once a year, perhaps at Christmas—but he was not interested at present.

At the beginning of 1903, another American collector made enquiries. Sibthorp told him that first refusal was already promised to another, but repeated his original move of naming a price so high that he considered it prohibitive—£10,000.

He felt obliged to inform Folger by personal letter, and on 23 January Folger once again cabled instructions to Railton: 'Buy without fail even at ten thousand cash but arrange time payments if you can.' When Sibthorp accepted, Folger had at last acquired the Vincent Folio, four years after his first attempt, and for $48,730.

HOW MANY COPIES DID FOLGER COLLECT?

It is not easy to define the Folger collection of First Folios as a precise number of copies. The number usually quoted is 79, because the shelves contain 79 collections of Folio leaves to which Folger himself gave numbers. The number of '79 copies' is sometimes followed by the words, 'and numerous fragments', but while that is certainly true, it overlooks the fact that some of the numbered copies contain fewer leaves than some of the groups of fragments. Hinman, who knew the collection more intimately than most, preferred to describe it as 'over eighty' copies, which is more realistic.

While only 13 of the copies are complete, and fewer than half have original title-pages, the status of most of the 79 numbered copies as 'copies' is beyond question. But the bound and numbered copy 66 contains little more than one-third of its original leaves, while four others are boxed collections of unbound, separate leaves from numerous

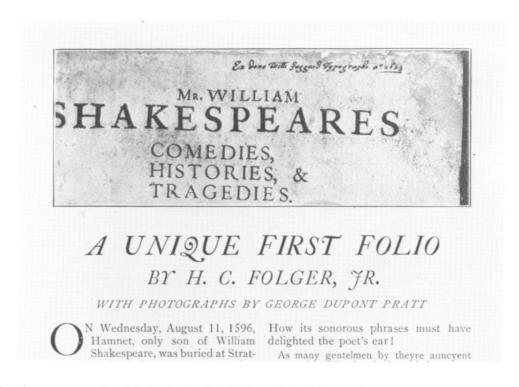

Henry Folger almost never wrote for publication, but he prized the Vincent Folio so highly that in 1907 he wrote a short illustrated article about it for The Outlook.

broken copies, and only one of those four collections is more than three-quarters complete.

The 'fragments' include three more assembled collections, each containing more leaves than copy 66. Two of those collections represent a collector's attempt to assemble two complete sets. The leaves are bound as separate plays or as groups of physically linked plays (in which one play ends, and the next begins, on the same leaf). The sets are identically bound, except that the best copy of each play or group is bound in red, and the other in green. Neither set is complete, and many of the plays have one or more leaves in facsimile, but the red set as a whole is more complete than four of the numbered copies, and even the green set is more complete than copies 66 and 74. Below them on the scale of completeness is an assortment of smaller fragments, including several dozen copies of a 'leaf book' entitled *A Noble Fragment*—a slim volume in praise of the Folio, with one original leaf bound into each copy.

To describe the collection as divided into 'copies' and 'fragments' is to suggest a clear distinction where none exists. It is a collection that includes both obvious copies and obvious fragments, but which ranges across a whole spectrum of completeness from perfect copies to defective single leaves. Whether or not the three major collections of uncatalogued leaves are ever formally defined and listed as 'copies', they deserve at least to be *counted* as copies—in which case the best strictly numerical answer to the question is 82. Because so many of them are so incomplete, that number may by some be considered both too high and too precise. But even if Hinman's 'over eighty' (or Lear's 'Fourscore and upward') is preferred, the fact remains that Forty Folio Folger earned his unprecedented nickname *twice*.

WHY SO MANY?

During Folger's lifetime there were many who criticized the way in which he cornered the market in First Folios. To most observers it seemed to be a case of hoarding for hoarding's sake, without any real purpose beyond a desire to own more copies than anyone else. There are still many who see the sheer magnitude of the collection as an absurdity, although few have ventured to define the dividing line between 'enough' and 'too many'.

The unparalleled value to scholarship of such an unprecedented collection was demonstrated in 1963 (at least to the satisfaction of most scholars), when Hinman's study was published. Hinman set out to do what Folger himself had hoped to begin, namely to compare the Folger copies in search of variants. But the opportunity to focus so closely on so many copies led him to unexpected discoveries, and persuaded him to attempt a reconstruction that has proved even more important than his list of variants. His work would not have been attempted, and could not have been completed, had it not been for the presence of so many Folios under a single roof.

Inevitably, perhaps, it has occasionally been argued since 1963 that the comparison has now been done, and the results have been so carefully documented that there is no further need for the copies to stay together. This exhibition itself can be offered as a smaller-scale demonstration that the value of the collection has yet to be fully explored. Nowhere else in the world is it possible to recount the history of so important a book by letting so many features of that history be illustrated by the book itself. And nowhere else in the world could the process of selecting copies to exhibit have yielded as many new 'finds' as are here exhibited, from the 'Nursery' *Hamlet* and the link between *Richard II* and Favyn's *Theater of Honour* at one end of the scale, to Thomas Bourne's security deposit and the binders' scissors at the other.

It is appropriate that such an incomparable book should have been made the focus of such an incomparable collection. The players' motives for collaborating in the publication of the First Folio included preserving Shakespeare's plays and leaving a memorial to his work, and the same motives prompted Folger to form his unrivalled collection. But in addition to being a memorial to Shakespeare, the collection is also a monument to the man who assembled it: the collector who, as Emily Folger so memorably understated it, 'rather specialized in First Folios'.